Miguel Ydígoras Fuentes

MY WAR
WITH
COMMUNISM

as told to Mario Rosenthal

PRENTICE-HALL, INC.
ENGLEWOOD CLIFFS, N. J.

CONTENTS

WHERE THERE IS BREATH THERE IS HOPE—
DUM SPIRO, SPERO

EVENTS that culminated in my involuntary retirement as the democratically elected President of Guatemala were diverse and the result of both political and economic factors.

I fought Castro-communism from the outset and from the first days of 1959 I was the victim of Fidel Castro's aggression. I frustrated his invasion of Panama in March, 1959; I broke off relations with his government in April, 1960; I withstood two military uprisings inspired by his money and his agents; I cooperated with anti-Castro groups to train two thousand Cubans and launched them against the Soviet bastion in the Caribbean; I put down an incipient civil war in March, April and May of 1962; I swung a submachine gun around my shoulder in November of 1962 and put down a rebellion of the Guatemalan Air Force.

Perhaps no other Latin American president faced more, and unceasing danger: seventeen national strikes, 685 terrorist sabotage bombs in the capital alone, two military rebellions, seven attempts on my life, and massive acts of terrorism.

But on the night of March 30, 1963, I was defeated by the enemy within: my own Minister of Defense, Colonel Enrique Peralta Azurdia, sent six tanks and 900 men to storm my residence, but I did not surrender until a tank crushed the weak doors of my home and aimed a cannon at my very face. It was impossible to resist with six loyal officers armed with submachine guns; I would have died in defense of the Constitution but too much innocent blood would have been shed. "Resign as president and take refuge in a friendly Embassy," I was told. "Never," I replied. "Lead me to the wall first."

Across the street was a rebellious barracks; all telephone lines had been cut; my residence was surrounded. But I refused to resign. As of this writing I am still constitutional President of Guatemala.

At 9:00 A.M. Sunday Morning, March 31, 1963, my wife and I were put on a Guatemalan Air Force transport plane and flown to Managua, Nicaragua. The first measures of the *de facto* government that ousted me were to dissolve Congress, outlaw all political parties, persecute presidential candidates driving them into exile, and to make the army the supreme power in the nation, investing the Minister of Defense with legislative and executive powers. An emergent democracy was ruthlessly suppressed.

The greatest harm suffered by Guatemala at the hands of Castro and which paved the way for my separation from the Presidency was the stagnation of business by unceasing acts of terrorism. Government revenues were decreased and unemployment was increased; the people became desperate. Castro-communism trained youth of both sexes who left the country over smuggler's trails, and received money and documents to continue their trips to Cuba and Russia from the Cuban Consuls in Mexico. Some flew to Merida while others reached islands off the Mexican coast, thus thousands of Guatemalans traveled to and from Cuba, returning as guerrillas, conspirators, terrorists, propaganda agents and paid assassins bent on magnicide. There was an intense traffic in small arms, explosives, propaganda and Communist literature.

These young men and women were thoroughly indoctrinated in every way during their trips behind the iron curtain. The most intelligent among them were dispatched to Prague, Moscow and Peking and received scientific training and on their return infiltrated the University student organizations, influencing thousands of non-Communists against the Guatemalan government.

Guatemala is an underdeveloped country—particularly in its tax system. There exists a very powerful oligarchy. The Communist Presidents Arévalo and Arbenz were unable to breach the fortress of these privileged few and, instead, used the oligarchy to enrich themselves. My government gave farmers and planters great advantages. The production of cotton was increased 400% and the exportation of other products was expanding.

But Guatemalans are timid businessmen because every change in our government has been followed by jailings, exile, violent death and the confiscation of wealth. I called these evils the Four National Horsemen of the Apocalypse and I tried to banish them from Guatemala. After I took office I returned all confiscated property still in government hands. I paid the price of properties that had already passed into other hands. I avoided creating exiles by every possible means; those who became exiles while I was president did so voluntarily. I did not condone one single execution, not even of those who were sentenced to pay the supreme penalty by the courts of law. I called this policy *"borron y cuenta nueva"* a Spanish phrase that means to forget the past and start anew.

Until November of 1962 Guatemala was one of the few countries in the world that had no income tax. Taxation on land is minimum and easily avoided by false evaluation of property. For years I attempted to pass tax reforms, only to be thwarted time and time again by powerful groups who cared only for themselves and not for their country, and who cleverly used the democratic systems I had established to block my proposed legislation.

Worker's pay in Guatemala has always been very low. Prior to my administration, the pro-Communist governments of Arévalo and Arbenz had made many concessions to labor, but these were not inspired by a desire to raise the workers permanently from their squalor. Rather they were aimed at slowly but surely destroying capitalism and free enterprise and dragging the country towards communism. The government of Castillo Armas revoked many of these concessions and my government sought an equilibrium between capital and labor in a new and equitable Code promulgated in July of 1961.

But it was impossible to raise the pay of the millions of agricultural workers who were chiefly dedicated to coffee, because this commodity was suffering a severe decline. If the planters had been unwilling to pay better wages when coffee was selling for $40, $50 and $60 per hundred weight, it was inconceivable that they would do so when coffee had dropped to $30.

I was not discouraged. I stimulated the growth of labor unions, and had experts from the Organization of American States study the problem of a minimum wage. Labor groups asked for needed reforms and as if by common consent there rose a clamor that enterprise share net profits with labor, something that I had established in State-owned industry. Businessmen and planters refused to give up a small percentage of their profits.

This was the situation with which I was confronted: the extreme Right determined—at any cost—never to pay taxes nor obey our new social reform laws demanded by the Charter of Bogota and the treaties of Punta del Este; traitors in the pay of the British conspiring to overthrow me to forestall talks on the

disputed territory of Belice (British Honduras) that I had bludg-
eoned the British into accepting; reds of every shade conspiring
to serve Soviet strategy, the most dangerous being those led by
Arévalo and Arbenz; enemies of the economic integration of Central America and the political union of the Isthmus working to
protect selfish interests; the United States looking on me with
suspicion because of the triumph of Communist propaganda
based on falsehoods that invaded even the most respected American periodicals; and, to all those diverse factors must be added the
ambitions of certain Colonels tempted by the bribes of the Right
and many low ranking officers tempted by the offers of the Left.

The political barometer fell dangerously low and indicated a
storm. The situation was made worse by the threat of an economic
crisis that had to be met immediately: national bankruptcy. Little
hope could be placed in the Alliance for Progress because it could
not move with the speed demanded by the internal situation of
Guatemala.

All this in the midst of a pre-election campaign to find my
legal successor. The situation was climaxed by the plans of the
extreme Left, the moderate Left, the Center and others, to use
the figure of former president Arévalo to unite all the extremists
and to again impose a Communist government on the country.
From Mexico, Arévalo announced his return to Guatemala.

I agreed to declare martial law and on March 25 I delegated
responsibility for the situation and the prevention of more dangerous incidents to the Minister of Defense, Colonel Enrique
Peralta Azurdia. But the sudden presence of Arévalo in Guatemala,
on the 29th of March, outwitting all the measures taken by the
Minister of Defense, Colonel Enrique Peralta Azurdia, sounded
the high note of a historic challenge for this man and his followers. They had no faith in the people of Guatemala; with no
historic precedent, nor basis in fact, they assumed that the entire
country would rise up like one man to support the leftist demagogue Arévalo. The mere fact that Arévalo was able to enter
Guatemala and evade the security measures set up by Defense
Minister Azurdia, and brazenly hold a press conference in a
secret place, imperiled Azurdia's prestige and political future.

It then became the moment for Peralta Azurdia to find a scape-
goat to cover up his inertia and weakness. Treason was the path
he chose and I was his victim. He believed the best expedient was
to turn against his chief and his friend, defying the Constitution

that he had sworn to defend, instead of redoubling his efforts in persecution of the real enemy of Guatemala. It was thus that he turned against me and at gun's point destroyed the intangible power of law and my democratic regime and drove me from my high office and my country, into exile.

The Communists are always alert to fall on an unstable government and this is why, in the first press conference after my exile, I urged friendly nations to recognize the *de facto* government of Guatemala to protect it against the possibility of a Communist take-over and to defend the advances achieved towards Central American integration. This was misinterpreted and used by my enemies to accuse me of having connived with Peralta Azurdia in planning my downfall. To those who know me and are familiar with the situation, this is so absurd that it does not even warrant comment.

Perhaps our ally the United States expected the Communists to assault the shores of Guatemala with jets and landing barges. But the actual attack came from within from the most ardent anti-Communist, who acted out of fear rather than wisdom and whose ill-conceived action may well boomerang, because every setback suffered by democratic representative government is a victory for communism.

These events have changed my role in the war with communism from that of the President of a nation to that of a private citizen. But as long as there is breath in my lungs—*dum spiro, spero*—I will pursue the battle with the same devotion.

My faith in representative democracy is unshaken. It is a system adapted to man's nature and not a system to which man must be adapted—usually through brutality—even if the man is destroyed in the process as has often happened under totalitarian systems. Only under systems based on personal liberty can man and societies attain their utmost achievements.

I am convinced that the people of Guatemala learned many lessons during the years they lived democratically under my government and that they would have demonstrated a measure of political maturity if they had been given the opportunity. I hope the experiences compiled in this brief volume will serve us all in our struggle against the common enemy.

Miguel Ydígoras Fuentes

Managua, Nicaragua
April 6, 1963

FOREWORD

REALITIES of the "cold" war in Latin America have been little realized in the United States. Or, for that matter, in a number of other Latin American countries. President Miguel Ydígoras Fuentes of Guatemala who has been commander in an active theatre of the "cold" war, here gives a first-hand, documented, blow by blow account of what it really means. He has performed a service in doing so, and his book deserves wide reading.

For those unacquainted with Central America, a word of introduction is in order. Guatemala, lying immediately south of Mexico, spans the Central American isthmus. More than half its population is Indian, much of them still living as Mayan Indians perhaps lived when the Spanish conquistadors arrived. President Ydígoras Fuentes' real political strength lies in the fact that most of the Indian population consider him as the Guatemalan political leader who has most knowledge of their problems, and is most interested in assisting them.

The allegedly "cold" war reached Central America at the close of World War II. The United States was still thinking of the Central American countries as "banana republics" useful chiefly as stage settings for Richard Harding Davis and O. Henry novelettes. Actually they were prompt targets of Soviet-Russian imperialism, aimed at long range against the United States. As early as 1947, a serious and almost successful bid was made to seize Costa Rica in which armed Communist elements were a principal force. They were defeated in open battle by José (Pépé) A. Figueres who later became President of Costa Rica (and who, in the fall of 1963, will be visiting professor at Harvard University).

In Guatemala, the serious struggle began after the fall (in 1944) of former Guatemalan dictator, General Jorge Ubico. Following a series of swift changes, Dr. Juan José Arévalo then became president. He was backed by a young colonel, Jacobo Arbenz, and by an anti-Communist, Francisco Arana. Arana was presently assassinated. Arbenz rapidly established himself first as power behind the Arévalo throne, then as government candidate for President and, in 1950, as President. Rapidly thereafter a Castro-style Communist take-over began. Communist arms and personnel were brought in from Czechoslovakia. After four years of increasing Communist take-over, an armed revolt, headed by Colonel Castillo Armas, brought about a popular uprising. Defeated, Jacobo Arbenz promptly fled to refuge behind the Iron Curtain (he later returned to and is currently reported in Cuba). Arbenz' chief Communist strategist, Che Guevara (an Argentine by birth) took refuge in Mexico, later joined the Castro force, became in 1959 the active instrument in betraying the 26th of July Cuban revolution into Russian-Communist hands. He is now a powerful element in the Castro regime.

Miguel Ydígoras Fuentes, in exile and out, alternated between one or another phase of active leadership, first in movements against Arévalo (who maintains he is not Communist and is still in the Guatemalan political picture), and later against Arévalo's successor, Arbenz. He was elected President of Guatemala in 1958. He successfully held his election against attempts to cancel it.

A few months after his election, the Castro revolution in Cuba succeeded. It was promptly betrayed by its leaders into a direct Communist take-over. Soon thereafter, Castro called for, got, and now has, men and arms from the Soviet Union. (At date of writing, though the rocket missiles and atomic warheads are supposed to have been eliminated, there is a Russian army of occupation in Cuba and the most powerful arsenal of weapons in Latin America.)

The Castro regime at once endeavored to duplicate its Cuban success in other countries. Guatemala was one of its first targets. This may have been because Che Guevara, formerly chief strategist for the displaced Guatemalan President Arbenz, wanted revenge for his defeat there. The exact methods used, the documentary intelligence and other records, not to mention a few dramatic side intrigues, are recounted by President Ydígoras Fuentes in this volume. The story is carried up to 1962. For all practical purposes, the Castro regime declared war on Guatemala, and carries it on now. Attacks have been almost continuous, carried out by the familiar methods of guerrilla invasion, internal conspiracy, attempted assassination and bribery of army officers.

President Ydígoras Fuentes' account is a fascinating drama. It is valuable as an historical record. It is significant, because it may explain certain facts to the American reader.

It explains why the men on the firing line in the "cold" war are all for the Alliance for Progress, and for social reform. But it also makes clear that good intentions, grants and loans and projects for permanent improvement do not stop bullets coming your way. Nor do they beat off guerrilla attacks armed, financed, directed and usually manned from outside. (In this case, the "outside" is Castro-Cuba, under Soviet military occupation.) It also explains why the Cuban talk of "defensive weapons" excites bitter laughter in Central America.

A Central American government which has the confidence of the bulk of its people—is believed by them to be working for their welfare—will be defended by its people. This has been indeed the chief factor maintaining President Ydígoras Fuentes in power, as it has proved decisive in maintaining his great contemporary, Romulo Betancourt, in power in Venezuela. Yet, even against that background, steady infiltrations of well-financed terrorists can make economic progress difficult —and assassination is always a possibility.

A leader in the "cold" war at once becomes "controversial." Communist propaganda attacks would make him so in any event. This is true in the case of President Ydígoras Fuentes. The author of this volume thus can not expect that it will not be challenged or that he will not be vilified in usual Communist fashion. His narrative, nevertheless, must be taken seriously. For American readers I make one observation. Latin Americans know what is going on in Latin America a great deal better than anyone else. Better, in fact, than the most scientific non-Latin American intelligence system. Making every allowance, correction and discount, what Latin Americans say about the forces and events in their own country deserves careful attention.

I am therefore glad to introduce President Ydígoras' volume to the American public.

Adolf A. Berle

March 1963
New York, New York

1

THE IRON CURTAIN
MOVES WEST

I

"BATISTA has resigned," Foreign Minister Unda Murillo informed me as he came into the dining room on January 1, 1959, for our traditional New Year's Day breakfast. "He has fled with all his ranking military and political supporters and deposited the presidency with the Chief Justice, Carlos M. Piedra." He extended a cablegram to me.

I waved him to the empty seat at my right and he greeted the other guests. A few minutes earlier I had walked down the corridor and for the first time the officers of the presidential general staff had greeted me with "Happy New Year." It was a fine, brisk morning. I had been President of Guatemala since March of the previous year. I was in high spirits and so were my guests but the Foreign Minister was tense.

"Happy New Year, Mr. Minister," I said, raising my glass of orange juice.

"Happy New Year, Mr. President," he replied, with a little bow, from his seat. But he kept his eyes on me inquiringly. The immediate question, of course, was that of recognition or non-recognition of the provisional Cuban government.

11

"We'll wait and see," I said. "There is no assurance that the provisional government will last; I doubt if it has the support of the United States. The State Department favors liberals," I smiled wryly; "loud-mouthed liberals; Piedra is far from that."

Chilo, the chief steward, ceremoniously placed the New Year's Day tamale on my plate, traditional for breakfast. As I was eating and thinking, the name of Fidel Castro came into my mind. Dr. Unda Murillo must have read my thoughts. He leaned towards me, and in an urgent, diplomatic whisper, said: "When I was Ambassador in Chile in 1957, I learned something about Fidel Castro."

He told me that a letter written by Fidel Castro to a Chilean senator had fallen into the hands of Chilean authorities, been photostated, and circulated widely. "In that letter," the Foreign Minister continued, "Castro made his political ideology known. He said that he was fighting for socialism because it was the salvation of the world. He made a lengthy defense of communism in both Russia and China and he ended the letter saying that if his revolution triumphed, he would impose communism on Cuba."

I watched subsequent events in Cuba with grave misgivings. As president of a country that had already suffered the tragic experience of communism, everything that happened in Cuba was pregnant with meaning to me.

Developments in Cuba after the collapse of Batista followed a vaguely familiar but alarmingly sinister pattern. I feared that Cuba would become the Communist base of operation in the Caribbean that Guatemala had been as late as 1954.

We did not publicize our fears, nor did we allow them to color our initial relations with the revolutionary government— a regime we decided to recognize, following the lead of the United States. Other governments may have been deceived by the nationalist disguise of Castro, he may have had his champions in high circles in other countries, but in Guatemala we knew him for what he was from the outset.

The mere fact that Ernest "Che" Guevara was his right-hand man was sufficient for us to consider Castro with the utmost suspicion. Guevara had been in Guatemala during the Arbenz pro-Communist government and while he had played but a minor role, he was known to be a "genuine" Communist. He fled the country with Arbenz and the other Communist leaders.

We saw in Castro's triumph the classic example of successful Communist maneuvering to use a national crisis to achieve power. Students of communism know that this strategy has been successfully applied by the ambitious Red leaders ever since Lenin.

We could see that Castro's "victory" was no victory in the true sense. It was a clever political coup; the reverse of the medal of Batista's failure. The Cuban nation repudiated Batista as the Russians had repudiated the Tsar; but it no more wanted Castro in 1959 than Russia had wanted Lenin in 1917.

Batista had been a cruel dictator, worse than any ever suffered in Guatemala. The year of 1958 saw the dissolution of his regime. His army and government met no overwhelming political or military defeats: they fell to pieces from internal corruption.

The climax came with the fraudulent elections of November 3, 1958, that gave a "victory at the polls" to a man who was recognized as Batista's tool, Andres Rivero Aguero. The people of Cuba realized that Batista meant to continue to rule from behind the scenes; it was common knowledge that he was to continue as commander-in-chief of the armed forces, after he stepped down as president.

The people of Cuba, like most Latin American peoples, are long-suffering. We have all endured dictatorships that seemed interminable, but always we see some ray of hope, some light on the horizon. When Batista thus "legally assured" his continued domination of Cuba, the Cuban people must have seen themselves being herded into a dead-end street, right up against a stone wall.

The United States had enormous interests in the sugar mills

in the Oriente Province of Cuba, where Castro was in control of the ports. In December of 1958 the American owners of the mills became gravely concerned over the fate of the 1958-59 sugar crop. It was obvious that under the circumstances, even if the crop were milled, they would have trouble shipping it out of Cuba.

The United States Ambassador to Cuba at that time, Mr. Earl E.T. Smith, made a trip to Washington in December. On December 7, 1958, the president of the United Fruit Company, Mr. Redmond, publicly asked Secretary of State John Foster Dulles to save the sugar crop of his company's Oriente mills.

From this moment things moved with extraordinary rapidity. When Ambassador Smith appeared before the Committee on the Judiciary of the U.S. Senate on August 27 and 30, 1960, he said, ". . . Upon instructions, I spent two hours and thirty-five minutes on December 17, 1958, with Batista, and I told him that the United States or rather, certain influential people in the United States, believed that he could no longer maintain effective control in Cuba, and that they believed it would avoid a great deal of further bloodshed if he were to retire."

When Senator Eastland, who was conducting the inquiry, asked if he had acted on instructions from the State Department, Ambassador Smith replied: "An ambassador never would have a conversation like that, sir, unless it was on instructions of the State Department."

Asked if he had been warning the State Department that Castro was a Marxist, Ambassador Smith replied affirmatively. Senator Eastland then said: "And yet in spite of that, of your advices to our government, you say that our government was primarily responsible in bringing Castro to power." To this, Ambassador Smith replied: "That is absolutely correct."

Senator Eastland then asked Ambassador Smith if he had ever discussed Castro with Mr. Roy Rubottom, the Undersecretary of State for Latin American Affairs, and what Mr.

Rubottom's attitude towards Castro was. Here Ambassador Smith replied: "In all due justice to Roy Rubottom, I think that Roy Rubottom was under terrific pressure from segments of the press, from certain members of Congress, from the avalanche of Castro sympathizers and revolutionary sympathizers who daily descended on the State Department, . . . and Rubottom may have taken the line of least resistance."

This was just another part of the Cuban picture. Basically, the situation that permitted Castro and the Communist Party to achieve power was as follows: the internal organization of the country a corrupt bureaucracy; guerrillas daily getting bolder; the Communist Party the only organized political group in the country. In April of 1958, eight months before Batista resigned, Castro issued a bold manifesto from his Sierra Maestra stronghold, calling for a general strike and warning Batista that "relentless war" would be waged against him. The general strike was a failure and the "relentless war" was never waged.

But by December of that year the picture had changed. The underground Communist Party, the Partido Socialista Popular, swung its support to Castro. In September the Communists had called for a united front against Batista. Castro had not enjoyed the support of the Communists when he first began to operate in Cuba. His invasion of Cuba from Mexico in 1957 had been supported by the Mexican Communist Lazaro Cardenas, but this did not mean that he had the approval of the Communist Party of the Soviet Union. Be that as it may, by December of 1958 Castro had the Communists on his side. A situation that could be used to the advantage of the politically trained Communist cadres had been created.

Batista fled on January 1, 1959; in the words of one cynical critic: "Batista had forty millions and he wanted to live to enjoy them."

Castro immediately moved in on Santiago de Cuba and in his first political address to the nation he said that Batista's sudden decision to resign had caught him by surprise. Nobody, not even Castro himself, had foreseen the rapid collapse of Batista. That is—except the Communist Party.

Despite his surprise, Castro acted quickly. With astonishing temerity and "revolutionary" legality he proclaimed Santiago to be the provisional capital of Cuba and appointed Manuel Urritia Lleo provisional president. Urritia immediately reciprocated by appointing Castro commander-in-chief of the armed forces.

Castro called for a general strike to repudiate the provisional government and Havana responded admirably, under the direction of the Communist Party. Batista was gone: no one wanted his stooge Piedra to remain in office. There was rioting and looting in Havana and while the provisional government made some attempt to come to terms with Castro these were unsuccessful.

Castro moved slowly on Havana, he did not arrive until January 9. His troops found a city littered with papers and filth. The ornate lobbies of the luxury hotels were filled with smashed potted plants and broken glass. He was received ecstatically by the Cubans and he said: "Power does not interest me, and I will not take it. From now on, the people are entirely free . . . ."

Communist strategists had many years to study their "near-success" in Guatemala, to analyze their mistakes and to ferret out their weaknesses and to lay their plans for the next opportunity. It came in Cuba on January 1, 1959. However, what had taken years in Guatemala was achieved in months in Cuba; and what was never accomplished in Guatemala: the total and absolute control of the government by the Communist Party, was ultimately achieved in Cuba. The Cuban Communists quickly destroyed the chief defense of democracy: the representative form of government under a democratic constitution.

I cannot conceive that any accomplishment of the Communist Party be mere luck. To be sure, fortuitous circumstances entered the picture. But taking advantage of the circumstances was not fortuitous, it was planned.

Communism may change its tactics. New leaders may rise up to replace the fallen. The plan of action may be altered. New objectives may be set up. But communism never modifies its fundamental beliefs, never is sincere with non-Communists, and will never renounce its ambition of ultimately converting the entire world to its political-economic system.

II

A mere month after Castro had assumed power, we were informed by our Embassy that the Partido Socialista Popular was infiltrating the Cuban labor unions and that its leaders, the known Communists, Blas Roca, Lazaro Peña and Juan Marinello, were very successful in their endeavors. We were told that there were Communists in the very heart of the Revolutionary Movement and those named were Raúl Castro, Camilo Cienfuegos, Ernesto Guevara and President Manuel Urritia Lleo himself.

My ambassador informed me in a memorandum as follows:

"The revolutionary movement had stated that the revolution had been carried out in order to give the people back their liberty, but this is not true insofar as freedom of expression is concerned, nor many other freedoms. It is hard to explain how the revolution (in whose name everything is done) can decree punishments for those who acted as censors for the Batista government when today it is obvious that the newspapers, regardless of their origin, background, or political position, do nothing but praise the government. Not one single line of criticism is published. In the wake of the mass executions which provoked unfavorable opinions in the press of the entire hemisphere, the Cuban press reacted violently and followed the government lead. The American press was invited to come to Cuba to see for itself what the true situation was. The local press defended the government and the decisions of the military courts, just as it defends everything the government does. The local press has gone as far as to attack the diplomatic corps when it demanded that the right of political asylum be fully respected in accord with existing treaties.

"Castro has said that the revolution is of the people and from this a series of internal political problems have arisen. These are being resolved in line with the policy of the new democracy that is being established in every class of society. As an example we have the reorganization of the university, the countless strikes demanding higher wages, the summary trials which have resulted in over a thousand executions, the dissolution of the army and the arrest of the greater part of all the officers. These are arrested first and charges are made later. If one court does not condemn, another is found that will.

"The present government has proclaimed an aggressive policy towards several other Latin American governments which are denounced as dictatorships by high officers of the present regime.

"Criminal laws with retroactive effect, a heinous and inhuman practice, have been passed. The property and wealth of all those in any way connected with the past regime have been confiscated; no matter how many generations were spent in creating them, and regardless of the origin. This has been done by brute force of arms and with no pretense of legality.

"None of the guarantees accorded to citizens of democratic regimes are in evidence. The most basic of all democratic rights, that of habeas corpus, does not exist. The special courts are passing judgement on those accused of 'war crimes' by applying a code decreed during the insurrection that has all the characteristics of an ex post facto law.

"Setting aside all considerations of a sentimental nature, the public trials afford to the eyes of an impartial observer very few of the guarantees of legality. Nothing of impartiality, equanimity, nor respect of the right of the accused to defend himself exists. The height of mockery is that in many instances the judge who presides is party to the very proceedings on which he will pass judgement.

"Freedom of education has been endangered by the Noll Law which cancels all study credits and degrees extended by public and private universities prior to the revolution during a certain period. This has paralyzed all the private universities. In short—the regime is unconstitutional in every department of government: Judicial, Fiscal, Treasury, Agriculture, Labor, and in every respect a mere travesty of democracy.

"Relations with other countries have become unfriendly, particularly with the United States. The revolutionaries always had arms from the United States, but these were exported clandestinely and in many instances arms shipments for Castro were held up by the authorities. Castro attacked the United States for having maintained military missions in Cuba while the country was bled with civil war. This is somewhat of an exaggeration, Castro never represented a real military threat to Batista.

"It was not until the fraudulent elections of November 3, 1958, that the entire country turned its back on Batista. At that moment all political parties became revolutionary movements.

"Despite the fact that the Cuban revolution has not as yet achieved domestic stability and is not consolidated on the home front, it has already made it flagrantly evident that its policy will be one of intervention in the internal affairs of other countries. The self-same Dr. Castro himself in his speeches has rudely attacked the Dominican Republic, Nicaragua and Paraguay, besides expressing his satisfaction that exiles should come to Cuba to organize their revolutionary activities, offering them every kind of aid, succor and assistance. It will not be long before the Guatemalan Communists in exile will make their way to this island to take advantage of these generous offers to help them reinstall their Communist government.

"Since it was the government of Venezuela that lent the most aid to the Cuban revolutionaries, the foreign policy of the country is aimed at strengthening relations between these two states. This was the real purpose behind Dr. Castro's recent trip to Venezuela, and is now confirmed by the declarations of Roberto Agramonte on his trip to Caracas for the inauguration of the new president.

"Other famous revolutionists who have received royal welcomes in Havana are Señor Gordon Ordaz, whose official visit to the Minister of State brought a protest from the Spanish Ambassador; Colonel Bayo, who is also a Republican Spaniard and Manuel Díaz Sotelo, a Nicaraguan revolutionary leader, have been in evidence here. I mention these gentlemen because they all represent forces aimed at disrupting governments.

"The labor movement, which had been restricted in its activities by the Batista government, has found complete freedom for development. While this is not to be censured, the determination with which every labor union is being infiltrated by Communists reminds me very much of our experience in Guatemala of 1944/1954. This is the real cause of the countless strikes and constant ferment among the laboring classes. . . ."

This was the first report from our Embassy in Havana after Fidel Castro came to power. How was it possible for us to have the least confidence in Fidel Castro's "revolutionary government"? We saw every symptom that had been in evidence in Guatemala ten years earlier when the Communists controlled our government. We immediately alerted our intelligence, looked to our borders, kept an eye on all who entered and left our country, and waited for the worst.

III

On February 15, 1959, two brothers, Raúl and Rolando Lorenzana, organized the first guerrilla movement in Guatemala aimed at overthrowing my government and opening the door for the Communist Party to rise to power.

The operation took place in the northern region of Guatemala, not far from the rail junction of Zacapa, which is also an important military base, near a farm called El Tempisque.

The region is known as the Sierra de las Minas and it was not only in the name that it resembled Cuba's Sierra Maestra. During the first week of April the following letter was shown to me (it had been intercepted in the mail):

La Habana, March 28, 1959

Señorita Magda Grajeda C.
31st Ave. 23-52 Aone 5
Guatemala

Dear Señorita Grajeda:

"I have seen your request published in *Bohemia* magazine for a souvenir from a Cuban soldier. It will be a pleasure for me to personally see that your desires are gratified, and that the other members of your Club, as well, receive a good quantity of buckles and insignias of the "26th of July Movement." These will reach you with a few words from my friend Commandant Castro Ruz, who is a great friend of the people of Guatemala. If I am able to be of service to you in the future, please call on me. While I will be happy to serve you during all the time I am here, very soon I plan to return to Guatemala to fight, so that we can all live in freedom, under true economic justice, that responds to the aspirations of the noble people of Guatemala.

Raúl Lorenzana

I transcribe below reports from my military intelligence on the guerrilla operations in the Sierra de las Minas section of Guatemala during February and March of 1959:

FEBRUARY 16, 1959

Two unknown Hondurans were reported in Chiquimula today enlisting men for a revolutionary movement in Honduras. They offered a wage of $3.00 per day and keep.

FEBRUARY 18, 1959

Suspicious movements of armed groups were reported in the region of the Copan ruins. They seem to be Honduran rebels but it is rumored that the movement is not directed against

Ramón Villeda Morales of Honduras but against Miguel Ydígoras Fuentes of Guatemala, according to agents infiltrated in the group. It is said that the operation has the support of Fidel Castro of Cuba and Rómulo Betancourt of Venezuela. The word is that once subversive operations commence within Guatemala similar operations will start on the Guatemala-Mexico border.

FEBRUARY 19, 1959

Several armed men arrived at *El Tempisque* farm on the night of the 15th in a pick-up truck. The truck carried a quantity of cartons which were unloaded. The men slept in the house of Apolinario Guzmán, rent cropper. The owner of the farm is Francisco Orellana Rivera. The armed men told Guzmán, the rent cropper, that they were executing a government mission. Guzmán pretended to believe them but secretly sent word to the owner of the property, who immediately advised the authorities. Very early on the morning of the 16th the armed men headed for the mountains, towards *El Tabacal*. They hired Guzmán and others as porters to carry the cartons which had been unloaded from their truck.

FEBRUARY 20, 1959

Gonzala Paz Vargas, military *Commisionado* of the hamlet of *Santiago Arriba,* reported that there was a camp of armed men in *El Tabacal;* that the men were all strangers, not known in the region, and that there was a constant influx of arms to their camp. It was rumored that the group was preparing an attack on the army base at Zacapa and that they expected air support from Guatemala City.

FEBRUARY 21, 1959

Men who had been hired to fight in Honduras and massed in the Copan ruins are deserting and sneaking back to their homes in Tecultan, Rio Hondo, Huite, El Jicaro and other villages in the Vacapa area. Three were picked up and are being held for questioning at the Zacapa army base. From their declarations it was learned that they had seen armed men, some dressed in khaki uniforms, others in green. It was said that the leader was called "Raúl."

FEBRUARY 24, 1959

Three guerrillas were captured yesterday at 15:00 hours by the military "commisionado" of El Lobo, in the Gualan district, with the assistance of his neighbors and volunteers. The prisoners are Alberto Ovando Quiñonez, Carlos Efraín Cofiño Samayoa and Eduardo Roberto Stackmann Fischer. They made the following declaration:

They came down from the hills to wait for Carlos Maselli, Cofiño Samayoa's brother-in-law, to borrow money from him because they had no funds. On the 15th of February they were at *El Tabacal* with Raúl and Rolando Lorenzana, and others whom they could not identify except as: "Otto," "Pemex," "Julio," "Palmitas," and "Eugenio." On the 14th the group arrived at El Rosario in a pick-up truck driven by Raúl Lorenzana and Bruno. They had left Salama at about nine in the morning. They had arrived at Salama from the farm *El Rincon* owned by the Lorenzana family. At first Raúl Lorenzana had recruited the men under the banner of fighting in Honduras to overthrow the government of Ramón Villeda Morales and offering them positions in the Honduran government after the movement had triumphed. Once they were in the mountains at *El Tabacal,* Raúl and Rolando Lorenzana told all the men that they were not going to Honduras, but that their object was to penetrate into the Sierra de las Minas with their arms and supplies to set up a guerrilla camp to combat the government of Miguel Ydígoras Fuentes. They were told that financial aid would be received from Cuba. Someone else was at that moment in El Salvador negotiating the purchase of a small airplane and more ammunition. Reinforcements were expected on

February 17. There was some discussion regarding the
strength of the garrison at the Zacapa Army Base. Rolando
Lorenzana estimated it to be 160 men. When the group
learned that the movement was against the government of
Guatemala and not against Honduras, it began to break up.
Raúl Lorenzana threatened to shoot anyone who deserted.
Those who showed the slightest sign of rebelliousness were
immediately disarmed and forced to work as porters. During
the first night nearly the entire force deserted, leaving only
the two leaders, Raúl and Rolando Lorenzana and two others
who remained faithful, identified as Bruno and Antonio.
Bruno was armed with a .22 sporting rifle; however, Antonio
had a Matzen machine gun and a Luger pistol; Raúl and
Rolando each had a machine gun, hand grenades, ammunition and also a 7.92 rifle. Raúl carried a brown bag and
wore a cloth insignia marked with the letters AN against a
red and green background. Both Raúl and Rolando had
compasses and carried olive green knapsacks.

FEBRUARY 26, 1959

El Rincon farm, of the Lorenzana brothers, was searched,
but nothing was found. The foreman said that Rolando Lorenzana and six others had left for the capital on February 3.
Raúl Lorenzana had not been to the farm for some time.

FEBRUARY 27, 1959

Guillermo Arroyo Ortiz and Cástulo López Aldana, two Indians, were captured, and declared as follows:

> Six men armed with machine guns fell on the town of Doña
> María on the 10th of February at 2200 hours and obliged
> several men to get out of bed to serve as porters. These
> were led to the North Atlantic Highway where they rendez-
> voused with a jeep. The driver was a dark man, with thick
> black moustache and beard; he was dressed in khaki and
> wore a khaki kepi. The jeep left in the direction of Guate-
> mala City. The forced porters and the others climbed

the mountains and penetrated into the hills for a distance
of about fifteen kilometers. They approached a sawmill and
saw between eighty and 100 men, some with beards and in
khaki uniforms; among these they were able to identify several. One of the six men who arrived with the porters and
who was called Manuel wore the insignia of a lieutenant of
the Guatemalan army. They noticed about ten large wooden
boxes, measuring about two feet wide by four feet long. The
involuntary porters deserted on the 12th of February and returned to their villages, despite the threats of death which
had been made if they did.

MARCH 4, 1959

Mopping up operations were ended today. Two units had been
detailed to go over the entire territory infiltrated by the guerrillas with a fine-tooth comb. The civilian population and the
military "commisionados" cooperated admirably.

IV

Very soon we had further word from our Ambassador in
Havana. A report dated April 17, 1959, read as follows:
"As pointed out previously the only organized political party
in Cuba today, which owes its existence to the strong underground which functioned during the entire anti-Batista movement, is the Communist Partido Socialista Popular. It came
out into the open the very day the revolution triumphed:
January 1, 1959. This organization is responsible for most
of the problems that today plague the nation; problems that
have been created with the full knowledge and consent of the
Revolutionary Government.
"Communism has infiltrated the key positions of the '26th
of July Movement,' and is active in the administration of
every labor union. It is public and notorious that the Communist Party has placed Communist leaders in every department of the revolutionary government. Most of these are

members of the '26th of July Movement,' but on the whole are completely unknown in Cuba and to the Cubans. While the Communists do not have a numerically powerful organization they have successfully occupied key positions in the revolution. From the safety of this political bastion they operate without any visible connection with the Communist Party itself. These gentlemen work within the government and the labor movements; some, who were already known to be Communists, continue active in the Party.

"Thus the Communist Party has won a strategic position in Cuban politics and can freely continue the labor of proselytizing and dissociation. The persons most often accused of being Communists are Raúl Castro, Commander-in-Chief of the Army; Ernest Guevara, Commandant of La Cabaña; Camilo Cienfuegos, Commandant of Camp Liberty (formerly Batista's stronghold, Camp Columbia); Engineer Enrique Otluski, Minister of Communications; Dr. Luis Orlando Rodríguez, Minister of the Interior; Dr. Armando Hart, Minister of Education; Dr. Armando Dorticos, who is drawing up the new revolutionary laws and enjoys the rank of Minister; Dr. Vicenta Antuna, Director of the National Institute of Culture; Camilo Cienfuegos' brother, who has been appointed cultural director of the revolutionary army. In addition to these, Commandant Almeida, head of Camp Managua and Commandant Almejeiras, director general of police, are said to be Communists.

"Unfortunately the revolution was deeply involved with communism and from the outset had many many Communists in its ranks. In addition the revolution has among its number many men who are filled with hatred and a burning desire for vengeance; men who have been hardened by years of suffering and privation: chief among these is Dr. Fidel Castro himself.

"It is hoped that Dr. Castro's announced trip to the United States will reduce the friction between the two countries, but it must be understood, before raising any hopes, that this friction has been created with the full knowledge of Dr. Fidel Castro, and that he himself has been instrumental in fomenting and aggravating it.

"The main purpose of the trip is to allow the financial experts, who will accompany the Prime Minister, to present their case to United States banks and to inform them of the true financial state in which Cuba finds itself. They are after large loans. According to informed sources, Cuba at this very moment needs some $300 million to put its economy in order.

["Yet when Fidel Castro addressed American newspaper editors in Washington, in April, 1959, he said: 'It is possible that many people believed we were coming here for money. I wish to explain that we didn't come for money. You should not think of our country as a beggar.']

"Also, official Washington circles expect Castro to repeat in public what he said privately to United States Ambassador to Cuba Philip Bonsal. He told Ambassador Bonsal, in a private interview, that in the event of a conflict Cuba would be on the side of the West; but in a public address on April 3, he said that Cuba would be neutral in the event of a conflict.

"When we consider Castro's great talent for saying one thing today and something quite the opposite tomorrow, it appears that he is using his private statement to Ambassador Bonsal to deceive the State Department into believing that his public utterance had no validity.

"The labor movement is daily more intimately identified with the Communist Party and receives the support of the revolutionary government, which is fully reciprocated. Despite this close relationship between labor and government, few advantages have issued to benefit the workers. Labor has been obliged to postpone its demands for higher wages and other reforms on the pretext that the precarious economic situation of Cuba calls for sacrifices; unemployment has not been reduced in the least degree, on the contrary, the number of workers without work prior to the revolution has been increased by those who have lost their employment as a consequence of the chaos created by the revolution.

"Obviously the Communist Party is extremely active. The policy follows closely that of Soviet Russia: the masses are kept subdued by promises that will never be kept. Every labor union is controlled by the Communist Party and daring anti-Communist groups within these unions have sent out an SOS to the government for relief from the pressure to which they are being subjected. They dare not mention the word 'Communist' but refer to the trouble-makers as 'dissociators.' However, their petitions fall on deaf ears within the revolutionary government and the opportunity is welcomed to persecute those who identify themselves as anti-Communists. Another alarming sign is that the CTC—the Cuban Confederation of Workers—is now completely dominated by the Communist Party. This organization is the central clearing house or nerve-center of the entire labor union movement in Cuba.

"When Castro cleverly took over the government in January, with the help of the underground Communist Party, he announced that all the executions would be over by March and that no more than 400 persons in all would suffer the ultimate penalty. We are now in the middle of April; the executions continue; already more than one thousand have been shot.

"The revolutionary army is still in the organizational phase. Impartial observers agree that every effort is being exerted to make it a Communist organization. It is the impression of most that it is not an army at all, and is distinguished from a faction or horde only by the identifying uniforms and the privilege of bearing arms. In truth; the army resembles what it really is: a group of guerrillas who have taken a city by storm. Their conduct is scandalous; they are slovenly in appearance; many have not shaven nor cut their hair for months or years. They seem to enjoy striking terror into the hearts of the people. All in all—Rome of Attila could not have been much worse: barbarians and blood!"

V

It was obvious that in Cuba the *revolution of the proletariat*, the first step as prescribed by the program of the Communist Party of the Soviet Union, was being successfully carried out in the Western Hemisphere. Castro's revolution had not ended on January 1, 1959. It had just begun.

The internal problems of the people of Cuba, of course, were very much their own. However, the Castro regime's policy of aggressive international proselytization soon gave his movement a standing in world affairs.

Castro took the pose of a "Liberator" and many ill-intentioned peoples took him at his word. "Tito" Arias accepted his help to attempt to overthrow the government of President Ernesto de la Guardia of Panama in April of 1959. Castro made it known that two ships had been dispatched to "invade" Panama. This was confirmed. The Panamanian government became alarmed and the question was discussed with the Military Command at the Canal Zone. The matter was not considered serious. However, President de la Guardia was not satisfied and he sent an emissary, Señor Fabrega, to request assistance from his neighbors. His pleas fell on deaf ears until he talked to me. I immediately asked the acting U.S. Chargé d'Affaires, Mr. Jamieson, to come to see us with the head of the U.S. Military Mission. These gentlemen took the same view as everyone else and said they would refer the matter to their superiors.

I could not see eye-to-eye with everyone else; I then told them—officially—that Guatemala was sending military aid to Panama because we considered our borders and the borders of Central America to extend to Panama.

Immediately our two C-47 Transports were loaded with war

supplies and sent to Panama. When they returned we sent them again, with a complement of officers and men, all volunteers. With them went pilots who were trained to handle any kind of craft—up to and including jet—and two crews for armored cars. They had been trained in the United States. If the need arose the equipment would be available, I was sure.

But this was not enough. The ships were sighted at sea. I sent a man to take pictures of a C-82 plane that was loading heavy oil-well equipment at our airport. This plane has many times the capacity of the C-47. He used a cheap camera and following instructions "sold" the information to Cuba's representative that ten or twenty such planes were daily taking off for Panama. The Cuban Ambassador wired Castro that "the entire Guatemalan Army was being sent to Panama." The Cubans tried to stop the ships but were unable to make radio contact. They then sent a plane to San José, Costa Rica and from there a man went in a light plane to the very invasion beach-head, where he instructed the "invaders" to surrender. This they did, as was reported, and it was my first victory over Castro-communism.

Our assistance to Panama not only forestalled a guerrilla war but brought Panama closer to Central America. Traditionally it was identified with South America and had been part of Colombia until the state seceded to sell the Canal Zone to the United States. As the result of a state visit made in July of 1959, when I was enthusiastically received, the people recognizing what we had done, I told them it would be better for them to be part of a united Central America with eleven million peoples than be alone between this nation and the Colombians who still harbored resentments for their secession.

Since then Panama has drawn closer to us, attended all our inter-Central American meetings, and it is my hope that she will soon become a part of our Central American common market that unites us economically, and I hope, will eventually bring about the political union.

VI

Relations between the United States and Cuba continued to deteriorate. Soon Castro was accusing the United States of permitting Florida to be converted into a military base for incursions against Cuba by air. The first defectors from the Castro regime fled the country and Commander Pedro Díaz Lanz made his famous accusation against Castro before a United States Senate investigating committee. When he was asked if he believed that Castro and the Communist Party were using the plea of a fight against dictators to cover up a Communist operation against other Latin American countries, he replied: "Yes, sir. I believe that in using that argument they can confuse people and . . . later on have what we have in Cuba. You know, we were fighting against a dictator and for democracy and freedom and most of the people did help, and finally what have they? What we have is another dictatorship *and* communism."

2

IGNORANCE–BIAS
AND THE COMINTERN

I

GUATEMALA, like most nations of the world, felt the first effects of communism shortly after the philosophy of Marx was transformed into the political system of Lenin.

As early as 1920 Communists were active in Guatemala. They allied themselves with conservatives to overthrow the dictatorship of Manuel Estrada Cabrera who had ruled in Guatemala with gun, spies, and prisons from 1898 to 1920. The first venture of the Communists into the politics of Guatemala served to favor the establishing of the labor union movement.

In the 1920's, after the downfall of Cabrera and during the administration of President Lázaro Chacon, 1926-1930, the first seeds of the labor union movement planted by the Communists began to bear fruit in Guatemala. President Chacon and some of his advisers became enthusiastic about the labor movement. With no idea of the nature of the problem nor understanding of its implications, they lent support to the strengthening of labor organizations. President Chacon financed the trips of several labor delegations to Communist Russia.

I spent four years in Europe and the United States attached to the Guatemalan Embassy in Washington and Paris and was a member of the Guatemalan Delegation to the Treaty of Versailles meetings. These short years in my formative period were to influence my outlook during my entire life. This was to be strengthened and to grow with the years. Unlike the traditional Latin American military man who becomes a president without setting foot outside of his own country and whose rationale is limited to the concepts, often narrow, that exist between the borders of his own nation, I was fortunate to be able to travel and to spend a good part of my adult life outside of Guatemala.

When I was subsequently appointed governor of the Department of Retalhuleu, I found conditions exactly the same as I had seen them fifteen or twenty years earlier. The inhabitants were divided into two groups: the haves and the have-nots, the former being a powerful minority. The have-nots—day laborers, agricultural workers and "colonos" who lived on the farms of their masters—formed one group. The landowners, merchants and high government employees made up the other. When one of the groups sided with the government, the other immediately took the opposite view.

During Chacon's administration the wealthy class was in favor of the government and gave it full support. The workers opposed the government but sought its assistance indirectly. As Governor of Retalhuleu I came into contact with all classes. The laboring class was constantly making requests for money to support its labor organizations. After the return of their "leaders" from visits to Russia, waves of enthusiasm swept over them.

At about this time, there fell into my hands a book entitled *White Communism* by someone whose name was Tirado. It was published in Buenos Aires, which at that time was the stronghold for communism in Latin America. The book spoke in grave terms of "White Communism" as opposed to "Red Communism" and developed a theory that almost incorporated

"White Communism" into the Catholic Church and proved its apostolic origin. When I informed my superiors of this, because it seemed to me a dangerous weapon among the credulous Indians of Guatemala who will follow a priest and a cross in any direction, I was instructed to accept the "White" Communists as "good" Communists and to lend them all the assistance I could. But they never won my confidence and I kept my eye on them.

II

In 1931 an officer of the old school, educated in the tradition of the iron fist and impatient with the niceties of democracy, became President of Guatemala: Jorge Ubico.

I consider Jorge Ubico to be more responsible for the rise of communism in Guatemala than any other single person. With a peculiar talent, he did everything to create dissatisfaction in the country. He was arbitrary, vain, blind to the true state of affairs in the country, supremely confident of his own judgement and suspicious of any other.

He was the inventor of the brilliant theory of depressing prices and wages in Guatemala to keep the cost of living abnormally low. He was an advocate of the infinitesimal wage and extremely low prices. This was his idea of a perfect economy.

I was director general of public works in his administration. The lot of my employees was often pathetically miserable. I was the chief of a group of desperate men. The department employed many men to drive its trucks and these were paid Q1.25 per day, equivalent to the same amount in United States currency. They were not paid for Sundays if they did not work, and despite the low cost of living their lot was far from happy. Because they were not allowed traveling expenses, whenever they were sent on a job outside of the capital, they were faced with the alternatives of going hungry themselves during the trip or depriving their families. A man who was obliged to make a trip of four or five days' duration faced a veritable Calvary. It was next to impossible for him to keep body and soul together.

I boldly suggested to the President that truck drivers be allowed traveling expenses on the basis of the distance traveled, so much per kilometer. General Ubico, who was an impressive looking man, with a harsh and haughty air, looked me squarely in the eye and said: "So! You too are a Communist!"

As director general of public works it was my obligation to report to the President once a week. On another visit he accused me of reading Communist literature. I wracked my brain to guess what he could be thinking of. It occurred to me that he might have heard that I was reading *Rerum Novarum,* the Papal encyclical on labor, written by Pope Leo XIII in 1891. I had it in my pocket and I immediately produced it and showed it to him. "You see," I said handing it to him, "I am reading a Papal encyclical on labor."

He took it and turned over a page or two with feeble curiosity. "Then it's true," he said. "There *was* a Communist Pope!"

III

Civil liberties were so restricted that it was not even possible to travel freely within the country. Freedom of enterprise was entirely relative and dependent on the will of the "General." There was, of course, no such thing as freedom of expression either in speaking or writing. Industry was incipient and barely in evidence. The lower classes received but miserable wages and agricultural laborers were practically bond-slaves. The middle class had no fields in which to labor and prosper. The country was truly stagnant. Guatemala needed a strong and healthy working and middle class, but Ubico said that the creation of new industries in Guatemala was tantamount to introducing communism into the country because no sooner would new industries be established than labor unions would be formed. In his mind this was synonymous with communism. It is impossible to detail all the obstacles placed in the road of freedom and progress in Guatemala at that time. Official discouragement of the growth of industry went hand in hand with a cruel system of police oppression.

The situation in Guatemala at that time was indeed that of "evolution or revolution," and resembled the proverbial boiler on which the safety valve was stuck. There was imminent danger of an explosion. And the explosion came. The famous Atlantic Charter, signed by the great champions of the West to bring about the defeat of Nazism and Fascism, brought great hopes to Guatemala of the possibility of overthrowing the terrifying dictatorship of Ubico. Inspired by the current of freedom that swept over the world, the people of Guatemala obliged the dictator to resign and he deposited the reins of government in the hands of three generals who were to rule as a triumvirate. Soon only one of the three remained, General Federico Ponce Vaides, superbly ill-fitted for the task of leading Guatemala along the path of evolution.

Thus the country remained in the grasp of "Ubico-ism" but without Ubico. The situation could not last and the inept "proxy" was overthrown by a second revolution, within a matter of months. This is celebrated today as the "20th of October," the turning point in the modern history of Guatemala.

It was a purely nationalist movement that asked for revindication of the rights of the people, something extraordinary and previously unheard of in Guatemala, but already matured in the conscience of the social experience of many other countries of Latin America.

During the revolution of October 20, 1944, the government of Federico Ponce Vaides was overthrown, and the entire diplomatic corps of Guatemala met at the United States Embassy to appoint the persons who were to mediate the

transfer of power. A junta made up of Major Francisco
Javier Arana, Jorge Toriello, and Captain Jacobo Arbenz
emerged—all of them youths, unknown in diplomatic and
high circles in Guatemala. Because of this the diplomatic
corps was loth to recognize the junta, fearing that it would
not comply with the terms that were being discussed, and
they asked for someone to guarantee the junta.

After several names were suggested, the Chilean Ambassador, Dr. Serrano, proposed mine, saying that I was an
engineer and that I had a clean record in both my civilian
and military career. I was accepted, and I in turn accepted
the responsibility. Thus my name was placed on that memorable document as the guarantor of the revolution.

Two days after the junta took office I was cunningly disposed of by being appointed the representative of the army to
the Inter-American Defense Commission in Washington, D.C.
Later, without being returned to Guatemala, I was appointed
Ambassador of Guatemala to Great Britain with instructions
to renew and revive Guatemala's claim on Belize (British
Honduras), the Guatemalan territory which Great Britain had
occupied for over a century.

IV

In a country where political freedom had been efficiently
suppressed for generations, it was no wonder that there were
no leaders to step forward to take the place of those who had
fallen before the advance of the times.

This left the field open to all those who had been expelled
from the country, victims of the Ubico dictatorship. Many had
indeed left to protect their lives and freedom; others had
wandered far afield in search of green pastures. These thousands of Guatemalan exiles, voluntary and otherwise, streamed
back to their homes. Not a few of them returned well indoctrinated in Communist disciplines from Mexico, Argentina,
Chile and even Russia. Often they were accompanied by their

mentors and these usually were masters in the art of rallying the masses, delivering demagogic appeals to the people, and organizing labor movements.

The revolution of the 20th of October responded to the clamor for reform but, lacking constructive abilities, it veered to the destructive left. The leaders of the revolution of October were unable to dominate the situation. For the first time in history the people of Guatemala had achieved political significance, and were beginning to enjoy certain rights. The leaders of the revolution were so intent on winning their support that the now politically important masses were wooed with privileges, concessions, bribes, and all other forms of corruption to which demagogic leaders resort. There was no attempt to establish standards of work, production or order, no thought of discipline. Old customs were destroyed and the family and community were undermined.

The first president to issue from the revolution was Dr. Juan José Arévalo. He found himself caught in a turbulent sea of opposing currents. Soon it became a whirlpool. The improvised president was obliged to compromise with many undesirable men, from the outset, to achieve a precarious political balance. His advisors came from many parts of the world, advocating methods that were obviously not in the national interest and which bore poisonous fruit for the country.

Colonel F. Javier Arana, who had been a prime force in the revolution of 1944, saw the danger and headed a reaction towards the center. He postulated himself from his post as chief of the armed forces for president. While he was a man of good and noble intentions he was not equipped to face the attacks that his attitude was to inspire. He was unable to conceive the depths to which his enemies would sink before seeing their plans frustrated. He was assassinated, shot by a band of criminals who were under the orders of Colonel Jacobo Arbenz, then Minister of Defense, and ambitious for the Presidency.

The death of Colonel Arana removed the last obstacle be-

tween the Arévalo government and the political ambitions of Arbenz. Soon the country was on a toboggan sliding down to the extreme Left. It was most natural that the gloomy and uncommunicative Arbenz should be the "administration's choice," for the coming elections.

During this political turmoil in my country, brought about by the revolution I had sponsored, I was busy being Ambassador to the Court of St. James.

V

The years I spent in England between 1944 and 1949 served me as a valuable lesson in functional democracy. That country was just emerging from a war which left it impoverished, but the democratic system was intact in every respect. I saw a nation enjoying liberty, exercising discipline and obeying the law. There the social revolution was taking place, perhaps not painlessly for those who were losing their estates and mansions, but at least, peacefully. I understood that it was not necessary to go to the extreme of destroying a system and way of life to better the lot of the people. It was also obvious that such changes had to come about slowly.

It was then that I witnessed the introduction of communism into Rumania, Bulgaria, Czechoslovakia, Poland and Hungary. The experience of these countries was quite different! Word began to seep back to London of the merciless process that was slowly and inexorably starving the people in countries liberated by Russia. Their governments were disrupted. Their agricultural systems destroyed by plans wherein the people, worn down by propaganda, hunger and desperation, said amongst themselves: "Our present system of government has failed: Nothing could be worse! We cannot continue to tolerate it. Let us seek a different system that will give us happiness!" And the people themselves began to ask for basic changes in their political systems. It was thus that those countries were slowly communized. Democratic rulers who did not flee were assassinated, or thrown from windows, like Jan Masaryk, to appear as suicides.

The United States finally opened its eyes and understood that it had crushed a monster called Nazism but under its very eyes another had sprung up—international communism. The weapons of communism were quite different. Communism works like a fox, conspires, seduces, corrupts, and generously offers all that it will never give. It offers everything, except oppression, dictatorship, loss of liberty and suppression of democracy, which are the only rewards it has bestowed on its "liberated" peoples. As a result of a revolutionary communistic "coup d'état" nothing remains of the framework of society within a once prosperous nation, except something called The State, in great, luminous letters, and an entity called the "citizen" who works for The State. To keep this unhappy entity from thinking even of redemption, The State denies the existence of God.

In the Communist totalitarian world there is a single authority. Absolute power over nations and peoples is given to a "leader," who stands not allegorically or mythically, but actually in all reality, at the top of a pyramid. The "leader" is sustained by unconditional and faithful retainers who conscientiously obey the orders they receive. These instructions travel down to the base, step by step, until the word of one man, at the pinnacle, becomes the law for millions of men, who form the colossal base of the monolithic structure known as the Communist Party. The Communist Party in turn, as we know, dominates the life, welfare and thoughts of every living being behind the Iron Curtain. Thus there is but one opinion, one thought and one direction.

The Soviet world has a definite plan of action designed to develop over periods of history. This program is a concrete plan of action that is to be fulfilled within specified "phases." If all the goals are not achieved within the set period, the program lapses, and a new program is set up that takes into consideration the weaknesses of the previous and renews with vigor the old goals and sets up new. The ideology and the entire system is at the command of the supreme leader. Whatever occasional glimpses of the plan the West has seen, it must be borne in mind that the chief article of faith and the fundamental and basic aim of the program of the Communist Party is world socialism. This implies the disappearance of the capitalist system from the face of the earth—to be achieved by fair means or foul.

What better proof can there be of the international conspiracy? In the "program," every single human activity, from shoe-making to promoting peaceful co-existence, is analyzed in the light of its usefulness for "building a system of world socialism."

VI

President Juan José Arévalo was "the voice in the wilderness" that heralded the coming to Guatemala of socialism. He brought with him the message of a strange philosophy which he called "spiritual socialism." Nobody understood what he was talking about, but his Trojan horse served as a wedge for the acceptance of Marxism by certain Guatemalan intellectuals and to pave the road for the flagrantly communistic administration of his successor, Jacobo Arbenz.

The Constitution of 1945 that had been drawn up immediately before Arévalo took office provided for a chief of the armed forces, a position which never existed before or since in Guatemala. Francisco Javier Arana in this post, was like the third party in a marital triangle. He was seen as the leader of the anti-Communist movement. Jacobo Arbenz, the Minister of Defense, was regarded as the leader of the Communist, or extreme Left group.

Towards the middle of 1948 Arana began to loom importantly in the political picture. It was decided that Arana was a threat to the leftist faction and that he should be eliminated.

Arana was ambushed and shot to death in his automobile. He was not alone, his driver and some other men who accompanied him survived. The driver was able, by some miracle, to obtain political asylum and to get out of the country. The other survivors have kept their mouths shut to this day. Arana's driver denounced five or six as guilty of the crime. These, instead of being arrested, soon were promoted.

The body of the chief of the armed forces was allowed to remain where it fell for five hours; then it disappeared for several days. It was only three or four days later when the whole affair had been re-written to suit Arévalo and Arbenz that the people of Guatemala were informed. These circumstances and the fact that during the next six years—throughout the balance of Arévalo's administration and during that of Arbenz—no attempt was ever made to investigate the murder, makes only one conclusion possible: the implication of both these former Presidents in the political assassination.

The death of Arana brought a violent reaction from the anti-Communist side, and his nearest friends embarked on an adventure to overthrow Arévalo by force of arms. They were inflamed with resentment against the government but they had no leader and Arbenz and Arévalo were not without their followers in the armed forces.

Although the followers of Arana—the Aranistas—formed a strong group in opposition to Arévalo's government, they were scattered, had no real organization, and were ineffective, despite their thirst for vengeance. When the Presidential elections of 1950 approached, this group, and the great majority of Guatemalans who were neither with the Left nor the Right, began to search for a leader.

During my entire public career, extending over a period of thirty-five years, from 1915 to 1950, I had never involved myself in politics. As a military officer I was obliged to be at the service of the government, and later served as a public official and diplomat.

The first letters and radiograms I received in London from

friends and acquaintances, inviting me to return to Guatemala
and to place myself at the head of an essentially anti-Communist political party, caught me by surprise. I permitted the
idea to rest in my mind and mentally prowled around it,
seeing it from every angle.

The letters were soon replaced by personal visits. I was
asked to place myself at the head of a political party that
would bring together all the anti-Communists of Guatemala.
The idea fascinated me; I was bewitched by thoughts of taking back to Guatemala all I had learned of freedom and
democracy in England. I prepared to return to Guatemala
because as the guarantor of the Guatemalan Revolution of
October, 1944 I had a grave civic responsibility.

VII

I requested a leave of absence from my government. It was
promptly refused.

This first pinprick of adversity ended any reservations that
may have hovered in my subconscious. It made me all the
more determined to oppose the Arévalo-Arbenz regime in
Guatemala.

I was a member of the International Olympic Games Committee, representing Guatemala. I got in touch with the president who was a personal friend and I asked to be accredited
as the official representative of the Committee to the Central
American Olympic Games, which I had helped to organize,
and which were to be held shortly in Guatemala. My appointment came by return mail and with this credential I
left London in March, 1950, to embark on the most thrilling
experience of my life.

At Merida, Mexico, the plane I was traveling on was
boarded by a Cuban general, who was also going to Guatemala
for the games as representative of the Cuban Olympic committee. We became acquainted at once and talked all the
while. When the plane landed in Guatemala I was told I

could not leave the plane. My new Cuban friend protested energetically and refused to leave the plane until I was also allowed to disembark. Thus it was that a Cuban general, whose name I do not recall, opened the doors of my homeland to me.

When I stepped out on the landing platform, I found an enormous number of people waiting for me, cheering and carrying standards that proclaimed me as their leader who would lead them to victory. From that moment I had no difficulty making speeches and coming to an understanding with my followers.

I then enrolled in the kindergarten of Guatemalan politics. I fought tooth and nail from early March until July 18, 1950. President Arévalo had offered Guatemala free and legal elections. But when it was realized that most of Guatemala would vote for me and the elections would go against the "administration's choice," Jacobo Arbenz, the elections became corrupt.

The persecution by the government of myself and my followers was ruthless. Many of my partisans were assassinated. A political demonstration in my favor filled the main streets of Guatemala and the Central Plaza before the National Palace. The government declared a state of siege and my closest friends, my family, and I had to take refuge to defend our lives.

The intention of the government to socialize Guatemala was notorious and public; Communist leaders occupied key positions in the government. The newspapers and radio stations, most of which were at the service of Arévalo because of his generous distribution of public funds, roared at me as the reincarnation of Jorge Ubico, I was called a regressive reactionary and President Arévalo himself gave us the epithet of "crabs," an animal that presumably walks backwards.

I was obliged to send my family out of the country, to neighboring El Salvador. I went into hiding and changed my quarters every four or five days. While I was not a criminal and there were no charges against me, and my party was still recognized, I was forced to conduct my campaign from the "underground." This manner of conducting a political campaign was indeed ludicrous. It might have inspired laughter, if it had not borne the seeds of tragedy.

The government persecution was such that a horde fell on our party headquarters and made off with the roof, the windows, the doors, the very tiles from the floor, to say nothing of our few pieces of furniture and our safe, where we had but a few pesos. For two months my life hung by a hair. The government sent squads of police to surround entire city blocks and searched house by house, room by room, closet by closet, wardrobe by wardrobe, looking for General Ydígoras Fuentes.

I had several close calls and twice I was actually found and confronted by my persecutors. It is most incredible that when the search parties did find me—twice—the officer in charge, in mufti of course, gave me a military salute, shook my hand and left. One even pressed a firearm on me to defend myself. If either of these men had not been true to Guatemala and disloyal to Arévalo, I would not be writing these words.

Five days before the elections, Major Castillo Armas attacked one of the military garrisons of the capital. The attempt was singularly unsuccessful. Castillo Armas thought that his men would be met by accomplices, instead they were met with machine gun fire. While Castillo Armas survived by a miracle, literally taken from the very burial pit to the prison hospital, most of his followers were killed.

I was naturally in sympathy with any movement against the threat that loomed over Guatemala, but I had nothing to do with this attempted coup. Nevertheless, the government issued a warrant for my arrest. Heretofore their attentions had been purely informal, but now the government ordered the wholesale arrest of all the committee leaders of my party throughout the country, in every village and hamlet they were imprisoned. Their arrest left our party without a single representative in the field, without any witnesses at the voting tables. The government of course controlled the telegraph system and it was next to impossible for us to appoint substitutes, from our hiding place. It was thus that I stood for office in my first election—sought by the police and all my principal supporters either in jail or hiding.

I am convinced that my party won at the polls, despite the machinations of Arbenz and Arévalo. The elections were held during three successive days, November 11, 12 and 13, 1950. We knew that 100 trucks were traveling over the country during these days, each carrying a load of forty or fifty Indians, who voted as often as time and distance permitted. The votes were counted and Colonel Arbenz was declared the victor. The next day a fire broke out in the building where the votes from all over the country had been taken to be counted. The fire destroyed the building and, of course, all the ballots.

Arévalo proclaimed that the "administration's choice" had triumphed. I was able to leave Guatemala alive only because of the protection afforded me by a foreign embassy. There was nothing further for me to do in Guatemala.

VIII

Arbenz was a bad president and a dangerous person.

After his fraudulent elections he was sworn into office. From the earliest days he was surrounded by sinister men of leftist leanings, many of whom had been expelled from Central America and other countries. Guatemala became the mecca for every Marxist, Leninist, Stalinist, and Communist in Latin America.

The first step in the Soviet program of communization of the country was set in motion by the Communist Party. The front ranks were filled by poorly paid intellectuals—school teachers, newspapermen, writers, artists, unsuccessful professionals, lawyers, doctors or dentists, politicians who had never won an election. Soon the university students, labor unions and even the primary and high school children, with their teachers, were thoroughly indoctrinated and organized into a well-knit front.

Laws that had their roots in Marxist theory were passed and a Muscovite constitution was prepared for the country.

Among all the murmurings, predictions, alarm and speculation, one voice of clear warning resounded through the hills and valleys of Guatemala, the voice of the Church. A priest, the Archbishop of Guatemala, Rossell Arellana, risked his life by traveling throughout the country with the replica of a crucifix, the Christ of Esquipulas, in his hands.

agents of the C.I.A. They said that I was a popular figure in Guatemala and that they wanted to lend their assistance to overthrow Arbenz. When I asked their conditions for the assistance I found them unacceptable. Among other things I was to promise to favor the United Fruit Company and the International Railways of Central America; to destroy the railroad workers labor union; to suspend claims against Great Britain for the Belize territory; to establish a strong-arm government, on the style of Ubico. Further, I was to pay back every cent that was invested in the undertaking on the basis of accounts that would be presented to me afterwards. I told them that I would have to be given time to prepare my conditions, as theirs seemed to me to be unfavorable to Guatemala. They withdrew, promising to return; I never saw them again.

Meanwhile, Colonel Castillo Armas, who had been miraculously spared his life in his attack on the Aurora Air Force Base in Guatemala City a few days before the 1950 elections, had worked another miracle in managing to escape from the penitentiary. He found political asylum in the Colombian Embassy, and under the Colombian flag was able to leave Guatemala. From Colombia he went to the Honduras.

I was soon informed that Colonel Castillo Armas had been chosen as the person most fit to lead the military operation against Arbenz and that a mutual agreement had been achieved. I was then invited to pact with the Colonel.

Colonel Castillo Armas then paid me a visit in San Salvador. He told me that he had the promise of assistance from official United States agencies, an offer from the Government of Honduras to give him asylum and allow the common border with Guatemala to be used for the attack, that the Government of Nicaragua had also offered him arms and bases for training troops, and that Generalissimo Rafael Leonidas Trujillo of Santo Domingo was generously supplying him with substantial economic assistance and large quantities of arms. We agreed on conditions and the "gentlemen's pact," as it was later called, was drawn up and signed.

The most important point in the "gentlemen's pact," and one that I insisted be included, was regarding free elections in Guatemala. It provided that once the illegitimate government of Arbenz was overthrown, that free and legal elections were to be held in Guatemala for a new president. By some act of treachery, this document fell into the hands of Arbenz, and was published in a "white paper" denouncing the "imperialist threat to Guatemala."

II

My job was to inform all of my supporters in Guatemala that Castillo Armas and I were in complete agreement, that he was to lead an armed invasion to overthrow the Arbenz government, and immediately after to convoke free elections. I was to urge the fullest support, strategic and financial, to the movement. This I did, and this was the extent of my participation in the movement. However, it was important. Carlos Castillo Armas had no political following in Guatemala. He was hardly known, and then only as a daring "rebel" who had risked his life to overthrow Arévalo, but not under the banner of any known cause. And so we worked, each in his own field, for the success of our plans.

The armed movement commenced in the middle of June 1954. It was not the grandiose attack that had been announced, and it played a limited part in the overthrow of Jacobo Arbenz. It was the people of Guatemala themselves who made victory possible and brought defeat to communism. Neither the military nor the masses responded to the call to defend Arbenz. His government fell without glory and he crept to his shameful asylum in the Mexican Embassy, whence he abandoned his country, his friends, and his honor to continue his attacks on democracy from other Soviet bastions.

The army of liberation, led by Castillo Armas, instead of marching with victorious step to the capital, and capturing it by force, if necessary, bogged down a few miles beyond the Honduran frontier and the leaders went to San Salvador to hold fruitless, lengthy and disadvantageous talks with the provisional government that had succeeded Arbenz. This gave the enemies of democracy more than sufficient time to flee the country with the wealth they had accumulated, or to take asylum in different embassies. Many of the leaders who were responsible for thefts of enormous amounts from the public treasury, or horrible crimes of genocide that came to light soon after, were able to assure themselves comfort and security for the rest of their lives, thus setting a shining example to others, equally as ambitious, and who were to come after, that being a "leftist" was a profitable undertaking.

More serious was the opportunity extended to the Guatemalan Communist Party, the *Partido Guatemalteco de Trabajo*, to set up an underground organization. Colonel Castillo Armas in his less than triumphant entry into Guatemala emerged as number four in a directorate of five army men, three from the previous regime. After a heated struggle behind closed doors he emerged as the sole survivor of the directorate and the ruler of Guatemala, nor were they able to give the country a fundamental law, or constitution, suited to the period of transition from an epoch of pro-communism to legal democratic life.

III

I patiently waited for word from Castillo Armas regarding our "gentlemen's pact," and the promised "free elections." My patience at length was exhausted, for I heard nothing, and my next move was to approach the Guatemalan Embassy in San Salvador to solicit an entrance visa for my country.

This request was denied!

Nothing could have been clearer. From that moment I knew that the pact had been broken.

I had been used. So be it. I had no desire to participate further in the politics of Guatemala. But I was concerned with the recuperation of my army commission, which had been revoked during the Arbenz pro-Communist regime. I surreptitiously crossed the border and went personally to the Supreme Court to request a provisional writ while my case was reviewed. The magistrates of the high court of justice studiously and carefully—and materially—shut every door in my face. I was surrounded by uniformed police and special agents and the magistrates refused to see me and sent word that not only was it impossible for my plea to be heard, but with chicanery that spoke ill of the state of justice in Guatemala, informed me that they could not respond for my personal safety. Nevertheless, I was able to have them draw up and enter into the records of the court their historic decision. This was given to me for my ratification and signature. I took out a fountain pen and wrote in red ink: "The blood of General Miguel Ydígoras Fuentes falls on the criminal magistrates and their descendants."

By this time I had developed an acute political acumen, which meant a strong sense of survival. Therefore, before entering the Supreme Court, I had parked a powerful automobile directly before the doors, but directed against traffic on a one-way street. Knowing full well that I would be arrested the minute I stepped into the street, I had ordered the car's driver to keep its motor running, and when my business was over, I made a dash for the window, pushing aside those who stood in my path and dove through the glass— quite a feat at my age. We drove up the street and no one was able to pursue us, as the other vehicles were headed in the opposite and legal direction, and the street was too narrow for a u-turn.

I remained in hiding until I was able to get word to Colonel Castillo Armas. He professed ignorance of all these machinations and blamed those who surrounded him for my persecution. I told him that I considered the "gentlemen's pact" a thing of the past, that I had no political ambitions. This, however, was something easier said than proven, since my political supporters were indignantly searching me out and speaking loudly of the "iniquitous action" of Castillo Armas in not permitting free elections and of assuring himself the presidency on the basis of a plebiscite.

The Colonel offered me the Guatemalan Embassy in Colombia. I accepted the appointment and left the country within a few weeks.

The United States Ambassador to Guatemala during these days, the late Mr. John E. Peurifoy, has achieved fame in the United States press for his supposed participation in the overthrow of the Arbenz government.

I would like to make it clear that Mr. Peurifoy had no part in the preparation of the invasion carried out by Castillo Armas. He was a very astute man as he proved when he served his country as Ambassador to Greece. His part in Guatemala had been to induce certain army leaders to save their leader Arbenz by pretending to carry out a coup d'état. This, as everyone knows, was what happened. Arbenz resigned and deposited the presidency with a military junta.

Mr. Peurifoy took advantage of events to bring himself into the public eye and call the attention of the State Department to his "brilliant" intervention by holding a press conference, once the invasion had started, and insinuating himself to be one of the most important actors in the drama. He was in constant contact with foreign correspondents throughout the campaign and this of course created the illusion that he had some mysterious participation.

What he did do was to attempt to impose the military junta, to whom the Communist Arbenz had resigned power, over the person of Castillo Armas. This was achieved in a series of conferences held in San Salvador. There a provisional government was formed that put Castillo Armas in fourth place in a five-man junta.

Mr. Peurifoy is also credited with having intervened in the San Salvador talks and made them a success. I know that the final agreements were reached because of the pressure exerted by former President Oscar Osorio of El Salvador, who agreed in principle with Peurifoy's views.

I had a last talk with Mr. Peurifoy just before I left for Colombia. I expressed my doubts as to the wisdom of suppressing elections and substituting a plebiscite. It seemed to me a shame that the new government would not begin its work on a democratic base. I told him that Castillo Armas, because of his popularity, would certainly have been the victor in an election at that time.

"Democracy," Mr. Peurifoy responded. "There will be no democracy in Guatemala, nor free press." This was certainly his personal opinion, I said to myself, and did not reflect the opinion of the State Department.

Before again abandoning Guatemala, I called my followers together and told them, in the words of a bull fighter who quits the ring, that: "I was cutting off my queue." I made it clear that I was giving up politics and suggested that they cooperate with Castillo Armas. Those who did not want to, of course, were free to join other parties.

In Colombia, I consistently refused to reply to any mail of a political nature. But I watched the developments in my country from a distance. It was more than clear to me that the constitution which was being drawn up, and whose authors had confirmed Castillo Armas in office for six years as their first act, was not what the country needed. Still, the Constitution of 1956 was adopted and the country entered a period of relative calm.

In July of 1957 President Castillo Armas was murdered.

It was alleged that the assassin—one of his personal guards—was a member of the Communist Party. It was also rumored that Armas' own followers had betrayed him because he would not allow them to exploit the people.

IV

Messages and letters reached me from Guatemala urging me to return. There was no question in my mind; I made preparations to return to Guatemala to renew my battle against communism. I knew that this time I would find the Com-

munists shoulder to shoulder with the officials of the government, who for the most part were followers of Castillo Armas
and anti-Communists. A rare coalition.

This was a new adventure. Eight years had passed since
I had arrived in Guatemala from London to fight for democracy in Guatemala. It was time to return.

The government of Castillo Armas, known as "the liberation," had failed to attack communism at the roots. The only
measures taken were those incorporated in the transitory provision of the Constitution of 1956 (number six) which ex-
cluded from Guatemala for a period of five years all those
who had abruptly abandoned the country after the fall of
Arbenz, and who were implicated in the Communist movement. The period was up on March 1, 1961.

Two things struck me on my return to Guatemala: the
gravity of the situation and the cause for optimism.

The situation was grave because the remnants of Castillo
Armas' political party was without a leader. Coffee, the life
blood of Guatemala, and which sets the pace of the economy,
had been falling like a leaf in the wind. The Communist
movement was forging ahead. On all sides I saw signs of
morbid dissolution and corruption of the fundamental principles of ethics, reason and justice.

On the other hand, the bright part, for me, was the welcome
I received on my arrival. Over a hundred thousand persons
stormed the airport, and this in a city of but 350,000. I was
not returning preceded by the fame of a conquering chieftain.
The reception I received was from a people harried and
fearful, seeking a leader. From the outset it was obvious that
no one wanted or desired either a dictatorship of the Right
or of the Left. What was wanted was a government that
would respect the principles of liberty and democracy.

The first welcome from the government came less than two
hours after I set foot in Guatemala. A Molotov bomb was
thrown at my wife and myself as we were escorted by the
welcoming parade on its way to Guatemala City. A rain of

stones fell on us and the automobile in which we rode careened
and crashed into a truck that was parked fifty feet ahead. My
wife suffered several broken ribs and I was badly shaken. But
this only angered the people and inclined them more in my
favor.

As in my previous political campaign, we had little money,
and were in danger of drowning in the flood of money that the
government loosed from the national treasury and from funds
that certain foreign enterprises placed at the disposition of
the heirs of Castillo Armas, the same who had financed his
"army of liberation."

It was the day of election. Voting was by printed ballot
and these had been distributed to the polls in limited quantities. The supporters of the government candidate had been
instructed to fall in line hours before the official opening.
Sufficient ballots were supplied at each table to serve the expected number of "partisans."

The result was inevitable—the government won by an overwhelming majority. What followed was something never before witnessed in Guatemala, and rarely, if ever, in other
Latin American countries.

I had vowed that I would not accept a fraudulent defeat.
My faith was in the people and I had to test their faith in me.
I called on them to protest the electoral farce. One hundred
thousand strong, they accompanied me four nights and three
days in the Central Plaza, before the National Palace, in rain
and storm. Before the compact mass of determined humanity
the provisional government was helpless. Even while we were
assembled the Provisional President resigned and a military
junta of three colonels stepped out on the balcony to an-
nounce this to us. Their spokesman said that they would
govern for eighteen months in order to reorganize the country.

A spokesman of the people raised his voice and said: "You
will not govern for eighteen months, nor eighteen days, we
will give you exactly eighteen hours to comply with the Constitution of Guatemala and swear in as president the second

presidential designate, Señor Guillermo Flores Avendaño. We will call on him to hold free and just elections and to declare that the past fraudulent elections be null and void."

Our conditions were accepted, Avendaño was sworn in as provisional president and the deposed administration, together with "their candidate," left the country temporarily. At the airport they declared to reporters that they were going to Mexico "for their health." However, after the long and tiring conflict I was right back where I started—a candidate with a campaign before him!

The machinery of the opposition to me was still intact, no longer within the government, but throughout the nation. These continued on, not only with funds stolen from the public treasury, but with money that reached them from outside the country, from powerful interests that did not want to see me as president of Guatemala. These knew that they could never bring me to my knees, and that if I became president I would be free and independent and committed only to the people of Guatemala, and with no obligations to particular and private interests.

At this time something disastrous for the future of Guatemala occurred. My opponents reasoned that I had achieved such a strong following because I had the support of the underground Communist Party. This was completely false. However, they decided to take these votes from me by founding a new leftist party; great quantities of money were placed in the hands of leaders who leaned towards the Left and the Communist Partido Revolucionario was duly born.

Many supporters of the liberation movement of Castillo Armas had lost faith in their party and they joined the Partido Revolucionario believing that the votes of the Left would carry them to victory. The elections were free and legal, although the old regime still exerted certain influence in distant and heavily populated districts. My party won a plurality in the elections, we got the most votes, but not the absolute majority needed to win the elections. The matter then became a second degree election, to be decided by the honorable members of Congress, dominated by an overwhelming majority of the old party I had been fighting at the polls.

However, on this occasion they showed themselves impartial and adjudicated victory to the candidate who had received the most votes—myself. I was elected president in this second degree election, and a few days later, proclaimed President of Guatemala.

V

Before Congress had given me the victory, and while the matter still hung in the balance, I had had a strange experience which I made known to the nation. It may have been a factor in the action of the congressmen.

A visiting American had requested a private and personal interview with me. Curious, I accepted. When we were alone, he said his name was Karr, and opened an enormous suitcase and began to take out packages of United States currency. He kept putting packages of money on the table until he confronted me with a half million dollars in cash.

"This is yours," he said. "But you must withdraw from the election."

I denounced the attempted bribe over radio, television, and in the newspapers. I suspected the true origin of the money, but lacking documentary evidence, I chose to blame it on an imaginary oil company.

VI

As President-elect I decided to travel. Thus in the last days of February, 1958, immediately before taking office in March, I visited all of Central America, Mexico, and the United States.

The presidents of Honduras, El Salvador, Nicaragua and Costa Rica agreed to work with me for the reconstruction of the Union of Central America, which would make us a nation in the eyes of the world, not five disjointed segments such as we have been since 1840. I also received their pledges to support a regional military authority to safeguard all countries from the growing dangers of communism.

After a short visit to Mexico and exchange of protestations of friendship with President Adolfo Ruiz Cortines, I continued on to the United States, via Houston. I intended to use every means at my command to convince the Government of the United States that I was not its enemy, as they seemed to think. It was my greatest desire to have friendly relations with the great neighbor to the north.

However, the first thing that struck me was that the official U.S. Army transport placed at my service left Houston so late that we arrived in Washington after six P.M. Minutes before we landed the U.S. Chief of Protocol, who had met me in Houston and accompanied me in the plane, looked at his watch and said, "Sorry, there will be no honors because it is after six o'clock." It may seem a small thing—the absence of the twenty-one gun salute, the flags, the bands and the armed guards. I was embarrassed, not so much for myself but for my country.

I was received at Washington airport by Secretary of State John Foster Dulles and by the chargé d'affaires of Guatemala in Washington. With the best intentions in the world our representative handed me a slip of paper on which he had written some words that he considered would be most appropriate for me to pronounce on my arrival.

I tore the prepared speech into tiny bits. As soon as I descended from the plane I went directly to Mr. Dulles and shook hands with him, then I deliberately passed in front of six or seven other United States officials and greeted some personal friends with warmth and enthusiasm.

We then approached a stand which had been improvised and John Foster Dulles, who had all my admiration as one of the most valiant soldiers in the battle against communism, took the microphone and spoke briefly. "We welcome President-elect Ydígoras Fuentes. We want him to know that it is our desire to maintain our friendship with Guatemala, united to the efforts to fight the common enemy: international communism."

I replied with a brief expository speech, closing with the assurance that when I returned to Guatemala and was inaugurated as President I would organize a government on strict anti-Communist lines that would stand shoulder to shoulder with the United States at all times in the war with communism, and that possibly, on some few occasions, Guatemala would even be a few steps ahead.

When the brief ceremony was over we left by car. I sat at Mr. Dulles' right and my friend, Julio Asencio, chargé d'affaires of Guatemala, at Mr. Dulles' left. Mr. Dulles was silent. I also did not speak, waiting for the opportunity to break the thick ice. When we crossed the Potomac I was surprised to see an icebreaker in the stream. I pointed to the vessel and Mr. Dulles said, "Yes, that is an icebreaker." He then said that during the five preceding days the river had frozen over and that I was fortunate to have good weather during my visit. He then said a few words that I did not understand because I am slightly deaf in my left ear.

Mr. Asencio then asked me if I had heard what Mr. Dulles had said, and I shook my head and asked him to repeat it. "Mr. Dulles says that your words at the airport have dissipated the shadows and difficulties that have darkened your relations with the United States and that he wants to help you and your government."

This of course filled me with joy, until my conference with Roy Rubottom, Undersecretary of State for Latin America. It was the most remarkable meeting I had in Washington.

The first subject I took up with him was the matter of coffee. Provisional President Avendaño had requested that I suggest to the United States the possibility of regulating the importation of coffee to the country by import quotas. The United

States is the most important coffee market in the world. Mr. Rubottom smiled broadly when I said this. "What you want us to do is to turn the clock back several years; quotas are a war-time measure." Three years later, as a result of prolonged talks between the United States and Latin American coffee producers, the very system of quotas recommended by Guatemala was put into effect.

The necessity of strengthening our coastal defenses had always seemed important to me and among several matters I mentioned to him was the request to purchase two frigates, one for the Atlantic and one for the Pacific. Mr. Rubottom smiled, somewhat contemptuously.

"Perhaps," he said, "we could arrange to send you a few eight-foot patrol boats."

I later arranged to purchase a frigate from Sweden for $190,000, fully equipped with two naval .75's with a range of 40,000 feet, machine guns, sonar and radar. This vessel, for which Mr. Rubottom wanted to substitute an eight-foot patrol boat, two years later served to keep Cuban invaders from our coasts.

I then told Mr. Rubottom that I had reached an agreement with the other four presidents of Central America for establishing a political and military organization, modelled after NATO, to defend the Caribbean from the threats of communism, much more efficiently than was being done at that time. Our idea was to set up an independent office outside of Central America for the exchange of information. With the pledges of the four presidents, my own, and that of the United States, we would have six nations; and, certainly others would join.

Mr. Rubottom only frowned, muttered, and seemed to have hardly heard a word I said. My heart was heavy indeed for this was the man in whose hands rested the relations of my country with the great colossus of the North. Unfortunately none of my suggestions and recommendations were taken seriously. How different the situation and subsequent events in the Caribbean would have been, if Mr. Rubottom had looked on my suggestions with an open mind.

The same negative smile appeared on Mr. Rubottom's face when I was bold enough to suggest that the United States side with us in our controversy over the ownership of Belize with the British.

I kept my eyes and ears open in Washington and while I found many situations that puzzled me, other events cast light in dark corners and pieces began to fall into place.

The very next day I had an interview with Mr. Eugene Black, the president of the World Bank, in the Guatemalan Embassy. He told me bluntly that Guatemala could not expect one cent from the World Bank, nor from any other American bank. He gave me several reasons, the first was because Guatemala had no bi-lateral agreement for the guarantee of loans with the United States. The second was something that had nothing to do with the United States, but a debt dating back over 125 years involving England. A very complicated matter that had been settled in full according to the Guatemalan view but not according to the British. Third, I was informed that previous governments of Guatemala were indebted to certain American citizens and corporations. He also informed me that, acting on instructions from President Eisenhower, he had loaned Castillo Armas, then President of Guatemala, the amount of $18,200,000. He ruefully said that he would have been dismissed from his position by the board of directors if he had not been saved by a letter from President Eisenhower.

It was made plain that if Guatemala did not make good on oppressive claims, she would find the doors of the banks closed.

While in Washington, I received a visit from a group of sinister individuals, all dressed in black, who informed me that they were the representatives—and members of—a Washington law firm. They told me that they had financed the "liberation movement" of Castillo Armas, who had committed himself to certain payments. On his death he still owed them

$1,800,000, and as they considered me to be his "heir" they held me responsible for payment of this monumental amount.

If I refused to pay, they immediately warned me, I would be given the "silent treatment." I asked them what the "silent treatment" was, recalling an annual procession in Guatemala that takes place at night, illuminated by thousands of candles, which is called the "silent procession" and which is very impressive.

Without mincing words they told me that they were extremely influential in the State Department and even more in the United States press. If I refused them, any favorable news on my government would be suppressed; any damaging news would be played up.

I declined any responsibility for the debt and informed these gentlemen, suspecting that they were well aware of the fact already, that I was not the heir of Castillo Armas, that I indeed had swept from power those who attempted to rule in his place, the true heirs. I also told them that Castillo Armas had died under very suspicious circumstances.

"Not one cent will you get from me," I said roughly. It seemed to me that they were but vulgar blackmailers.

"Very well . . . you shall see," they promised.

VII

Next morning, President Eisenhower invited me to breakfast. Mr. Buchanan, chief of protocol, cautioned me that when the President took his napkin from his knees and placed it on the table, the interview was over. But I noticed that the President took his napkin in his hand several times, but always set it back on his lap.

When the breakfast was over President Eisenhower accompanied me to the door of the White House and there we were photographed together. It was a most significant photograph for me, because by some quirk President Eisenhower seems to be whispering something into my ear. But it was no

President Eisenhower seems to be whispering something into my ear. But it was no more than an optical illusion. How much it would have pleased me if he had said to me: "I am going to clear up some of the difficulties and misunderstandings you have with my fellow Americans" (Page 64).

The gravest problem was the rebirth of the Red movement in Guatemala (Page 80).

When I look back I am a little surprised that we took those first two bombs so seriously. They were to be followed by hundreds over a period of years (Page 89).

A handful of leftist students and Communist leaders had been able to use a labor conflict to paralyze the country (Page 99).

Terrorists bombings became more frequent. We captured suspects, the courts released them (Page 119).

"The government of Guatemala, but not its people . . . seems to ignore that in our country there is a large group of Cubans who were obliged to go into exile . . . These criminals are allowed . . . to install camps to train mercenaries that are financed and paid by Batista" (Page 101). *Note:* sign at rear right reads: "Helvetia, national shame." Helvetia was the chief Guatemalan training camp for anti-Castro troops.

The FUMN (teacher's union) was actively supported by the FUEGO (high school and primary school students' association). Nothing could be more ridiculous than . . . primary and high school students militating in a political movement . . . (Page 125).

The group was invited to choose one can at random. It was opened before their eyes and found to contain a hand grenade carefully packed in sawdust, just as we had said. All the other cans were opened. Each one yielded a grenade (Page 158).

When we were alone, Foreign Minister Unda Murillo told me that President Dorticos and his delegation had made declarations in Montevideo to newsmen and over the radio and television systems that very soon Guatemala and the other countries that had voted against Castro (at Punta del Este) would feel the consequences of their attitude (Page 182).

I went into the streets to show myself and to personally take the pulse of the public (page 197).

On the following afternoon, two expert saboteurs plied their trade on the gasoline storage tanks of the Esso Oil Company in Guatemala City (Page 206).

En la ciudad de Guatemala, siendo las 1:30 horas del día **veinti-**
ocho de Noviembre de mil novecientos sesenta y uno, se encuentra
presente en la ~~officina~~ , el señor JUAN FRANCIS-
CO BARRIOS DE LEÓN, quien dijo ser de 28 años de edad, soltero,-
tipógrafo, originario de Sibinal, del departamento de San Marcos,
y vecino de esta ciudad capital con domicilio en la 27 avenida -
27-66 de la zona 5, con cédula de vecindad A-1-178003 pero no la
porta, hijo de Rubén Ernesto Barrios y de Teresa de León, **habien**
do sido instado para que en el curso de la presente diligencia -
se conduzca nada mas con la verdad, y habiendo ofrecido hacerlo-
así se procedió a la siguiente indagatoria:

Manifiesta el señor Juan Francisco Barrios de León en forma ex-
pontánea, que es hermano del señor JULIO BARRIOS, Maestro y --
miembro del Partido Guatemalteco del Trabajo (PGT). Que él, Juan
Francisco principió a figurar en las filas de este partido, mas
o menos en el año 1953, cuya fecha exacta no recuerda, habiendo-
militado en primer lugar en ALIANZA DE LA JUVENTUD.-

Que a raíz de la caída del gobierno de Jacobo Arbenz Guzmán, sa-
~~lió exiliado~~ de Argentina, en donde permaneció por
~~...~~
~~en la...parte~~
foto de Cuba sin reconocer ~~a ninguna persona~~; en la No. 12, él mismo, -
Hernández Izaguirre, una intérprete estudiante universitaria y un-
latinoamericano; en la No. 13, una rusa y un dirigente latinoameri
cano en Zochi, Rusia; en la No. 14, el guatemalteco **miembro** del --
PGT, MAURO DE LEÓN, quien se le había olvidado mencionar como com-
pañero de viaje; en la No. 15, Sr. Hernández Izaguirre y Mauro de-
León; en la No. 16, Valdez Girón, dos delegados **latinoa**mericanos, -
una guía de la Universidad de Rusia y él mismo; en la No. 17, un-
uruguayo y él mismo.-

Leído que le fué lo escrito y bien enterado de su contenido y obj**e**
to, lo ratificó y firmó.

[firma]

Juan Francisco Barrios de León.

Nota: El interrogado señor Barrios, ~~pide~~
~~departamento, pero que se guarden las seguridades indispensables pa~~
~~ra su persona, y desea que su colaboración sea apreciada en su va~~
~~lor.-~~

[firma]

Juan Francisco Barrios de León.-

He was apprehended near the Mexican border and his declarations to
the authorities, a copy of which is shown above, relate his story of
traveling to Russia and China for indoctrination (Page 210).

REVOLVER:

1.- Colt 11-4 (Kilómetros)

2.-Canadiense tipo 9.

El empleo de los 2 es parecido.

1.-Colt.-Es arma semiautomática;la emplean oficiales.-Para distan
cia corta.

Componentes del arma.
calibre 11-4 (MM). Peso 1.1 kilo.

Primera velocidad 247 ms.,por segundo.Area de alcance efectivo:74 ms.
Siete cartuchos.
Se usan proyectiles corrientes.Los mismos que se usan en fusiles cana-
dienses.
Sacar el depósito de cartuchos por la aldaba.- Quitar la parte superior.-
Desarmar cañón.-Sacar el cerrojo.-Se desarma para limpiarla pieza por pieza.

EXTRUCTURA:

Cerrojo:muelle con su cápsula.
Caja de cerrojo.Disparador.Boca cañón.Peine.Siete tiros

CARABINA AMERICANA 7.62 mm.

La emplean oficiales y unidades especiales.Semiautomática.Sencilla y
liviana.
Alcance efectivo 74 metros.-300 yardas.-Peso: 2.3.kilos.-La velocidad:
670 ms.,segundos.-Depósito:15 proyectiles.-Proyectiles americanos 7.62.-Se
desarma para revisar y limpiar: 1°.-Quitar depósito.-2° Quitar cañón(torni
llo):-3°Quitar muelle.-4°Quitar carro corredizo.-5°Quitar disparador.-6°
Quitar cerrojo.

7.62 mm.,- 1903-1917.

Es un arma individual de infantería. Dispara las balas por separado.-
1903 pesa:3.95 kilos.- 1917 pesa:4.43 kilos.-Cargan 5 proyectiles.-1903
855 metros,segundos.- 1917, 880 metros,segundos.-Alcance efectivo 731 metros las dos.- Iguales proyectiles: 7.62 mm.,-InXXXXXXX

INFANTERIA.-

Tienen igual extructura,las 2 pueden llevar bayoneta.- 1903, 2,700 yardas,según graduación.- Largo: 1.76 metros (1917).- 1903, 1.10 metros.-

7.62. Tipo M.1.

Arma semiautomática,de uso individual.-Velocidad 823 metros segundo.-Pe-
so: 4.29 kilos.-8 proyectiles en el depósito.-Largo.1.07 cms.-1.10.-Alcance
efectivo 730 metros.-Los mismos proyectiles del fusil corriente e incendia-
rios.-Proyectiles perforadores.-Luminosos.- Se quita disparador,madera,mue-
lle,carro,cerrojo.- 8 proyectiles en estuche

The authorities found twenty-two handwritten blank books with careful
notes . . . the typed transcription totaled 95 legal size sheets. His notes,
transcribed from Notebook Number 2, comprise a complete manual on
demolition and sabotage . . . they contain formulae for preparing explosives, setting up chain explosions . . . It is a remarkable "do it yourself"
guerrilla handbook (Page 211).

more than an optical illusion. How much it would have pleased me if he had said to me: "I am going to try to clear up some of the difficulties and misunderstandings you have with my fellow Americans."

4

THE ATTACK BEGINS

I

On March 12, 1958, I was inaugurated President. I was not allowed to wear my uniform because even then I was still without any rank. I had been deprived of my commission by the Arbenz government and throughout the years of the Castillo Armas administration nothing had been done to revalidate my commission. One thing they could not take from me: my stripes as honor student and First Sergeant of the First Company of the Military Academy. Thus as a sergeant, I became President of Guatemala.

It had been a long struggle—from 1950 to 1958—but at length my destiny was to be fulfilled. I swore fealty to the Constitution and in my heart vowed that nothing would stand in the way of my earnest desire to see democracy a reality in Guatemala.

I knew full well that the road ahead was hard; but in the most extravagant flights of imagination I was unable to conceive how truly difficult the path would be. And thankless . . . to a great extent. I had been betrayed in the past; but never as I was to be betrayed as President of Guatemala. But the darkest part was what neither, I nor anyone, could foresee: that one year after my inauguration we were to have a Communist outpost in the Caribbean, and this was the cruelest betrayal of all—for all Latin America was to suffer.

II

From the day I assumed the Presidency, like all presidents, and most people, I was confronted with problems that had no solution. All that could be done was to live with them. The chronic shortage of money was the first problem, the most serious problem, and the endemic problem. One that persists until this very moment, and becomes more acute as each day passes.

The economic problem arose from the drop in the price of coffee. It is strange how disaster can come to a country as the result of a reduction of one or two cents per pound for a commodity on the supermarket shelves.

The importance of coffee in the economy of my country cannot be exaggerated. It is the chief source of foreign exchange; it gives work to hundreds of thousands; it is the best client for machinery, bags, petroleum, transportation, insurance, buildings, roads, food and a hundred other items that make up our domestic commerce. It supports many other industries in the country. Above all, the national budget depends to a great extent on the export tax on coffee. This tax is assessed according to a sliding scale on the price at which the coffee is sold. In 1956, 1.358 million quintals* of coffee were sold on the world market for $90,883,209; and in 1958, the year I became President, 1.551 million quintals were sold for $77,501,802. Exports increased 15 per cent but sold for 20 per cent less. This not only curtailed the profits of the producers but also greatly decreased revenue.

While the reduction in revenue was not so marked during this first year of my government, another economic problem came to plague me.

Provisional President Flores Avendaño had done everything he could to protect the coffee industry. Guatemala had agreed, with other coffee-producing countries, to withhold from

*100 pounds.

market a certain percentage of the 1957-58 coffee crop, in an effort to defend the prices. President Flores Avendaño decided that only the State should suffer this blow and he decreed that the coffee production of the national farms (confiscated from enemy nationals at the end of World War II) should be stored and not sold. In this way private interests were hardly affected. This was indeed a political triumph but a disaster for the economy of Guatemala and a headache for me.

The national farms had a debt of between $10 and $12 million with the Bank of Guatemala, which it was given each year to cover maintenance and which was always settled when the crop was sold. But this year the crop was not sold and the debt could not be paid.

A government is no different from any other human organization. It takes money to keep it going and the money must come from somewhere. It doesn't grow on trees and it is not just a matter of running it off on the printing press. A family that has a number of fixed accounts which it must meet each month resembles a government. If the expenditures exceed the receipts, the head of the house is in a fix. My government had to meet expenses that ran between $8 and $9 million a month. If the money isn't there the expenses cannot be met. It is as simple as that. A government cannot just go out and raise money, like the head of a household. It cannot mortgage its assets or pawn its valuables. If it needs money the legislative body must approve any effort made by the executive to get it. If the legislative body doesn't want to cooperate, the president of a country can be in a very difficult position. This is just where I found myself at the outset of my administration.

Guatemala's economic situation had not been unfavorable up to that time. During President Arévalo's tenure, it so happened that coffee began to climb vertiginously. From $12 per quintal it went up to $25, $30, $40, $50, $60, $70 and even $80. This happy situation lasted until 1957.

The first blow against the price of coffee was directed by the United States investors, who poured vast amounts of money into Brazil, Indonesia and Central Africa for coffee planting. A coffee tree takes five years to mature; five years before it gives its first fruit. In 1957 the first cargoes of African coffee began to arrive on the European market.

In 1958 we received a visit from a commission from the International Monetary Fund. The Fund was established in Bretton Woods in 1942 and from it grew the International Bank for Reconstruction and Development: better known as the World Bank, of which Mr. Eugene Black, whom I mentioned in the previous chapter, was president.

A study of our economic situation resulted in a warning that our expenditures should be reduced by $5 million, by reduction in personnel in certain departments, but not in work projects, such as building and public roads. It was also recommended that we should increase our receipts by creating an income tax which would produce $5 or $6 million a year, and by thus increasing our receipts on the one hand and decreasing our expenditures by $5 million, we would have actually increased our available funds by $10 million. I was counseled to avoid internal loans because these had caused inflation wherever they had been used extensively. I was advised to borrow as much money as I could outside of Guatemala, on long and short term conditions.

I immediately put the matter up to the people. A vigorous publicity campaign placed the facts before everybody and we began to study the budget to put into effect the recommended reductions.

Unfortunately, the matter became a political question. Even those political parties that had helped me become president feared to support these necessary measures, afraid they would lose popularity. Congress flatly refused to approve the reduction in the budget. At the same time, it refused to approve the Income Tax Law, and another law which was to increase the land tax from 3 per cent to 6 per cent per $1,000 evaluation per year.

A certain percentage of the population of Guatemala—made up of professionals, entrepreneurs, businessmen, manufacturers, tradesmen, and government employees,—were enjoying a good standard of living and substantial incomes. All this numerous body were alarmed, because for the first time in the 500 years of Guatemalan history, their incomes were threatened with reductions by a direct tax, difficult to evade. They looked to the future and saw the modest demands of the proposed tax as a threat of prohibitive taxes in the future.

Such was the alarm created by the threat of "taxes" that heretofore peace-loving citizens and professionals, who had never paid one cent to help support the government, rallied behind every revolutionary suggestion. My name became anathema. So great were the repercussions, that the only benefit the country received for four years from my tax proposals were a series of uprisings, disorders, strikes and subversive movements—for the wily politicians of the Left, at the service of their masters in Moscow, soon turned the discontent to their advantage. Despite my repeated pleas to the legislators the proposed taxes were not approved until November 24, 1962, and provoked an uprising in which I barely escaped assassination. (See chapter 12.)

Meanwhile the price of coffee kept going down and there was a drain on our gold reserves. But as yet, no attempts were made to curb free buying and selling of dollars in Guatemala. The export tax on coffee dropped from $14 per quintal to $5.50, this being a direct reduction of government receipts. All other government receipts dropped proportionately, and it is estimated that government income decreased 35 per cent, more than one-third. Congress had not permitted us to reduce our expenditures: we were expected to work miracles. Less loyal persons might have taken recourse to printing paper money, and setting the economy of the country on the dangerous elevator of inflation. But our quetzal remained sound—it continued on a par with the U.S. dollar. Yet we faced a perilous situation.

Our economy unbalanced, general disillusionment among the people, unemployment increasing, growing unrest, and of course the government was blamed for everything. But what could we do? Look for outside loans.

Our financial experts prepared a "pilot plan" which needed $95 million to be put into effect and to set our house in order. We were honored with the visit of Dr. Milton Eisenhower in 1959 and we had several important meetings with him. I set our entire corps of financial experts, domestic and imported, bankers, statisticians, investors and businessmen for Guatemala in motion to prepare our recommendations for Dr. Eisenhower to place them in the hands of his brother, the President. When the work was given to him, and to his assistants, we were congratulated on the detailed study we had prepared. The memorandum was handed to Dr. Milton Eisenhower. That was the last we heard of it. When we consulted the State Department one year later we were told that Dr. Eisenhower had made reference to our plans in a speech before some obscure school in the Middle West.

We reduced the budget for 1959-60, but the congressmen increased it again, so there was little we could do. Our only recourse was to drop people from the government payrolls and this we did as much as we were legally permitted to do so.

The daily reports that I received from the Secretary of the Treasury (his was the first face I saw every morning at the breakfast table) alarmed me. The receipts from tax collections and import duties were greatly reduced. Many countries in South America had resolved their fiscal problems by printing paper money, but we in Guatemala had already been victims of this practice in 1897 and our economy had suffered the leprosy of this worthless money for a quarter of a century. The exchange had slowly risen from five pesos to the dollar to sixty to the dollar. Finally, after great sacrifices, in 1924, Guatemala had been able to stabilize her currency on a par with the U.S. dollar. We could not turn the clock back and destroy what had cost us so dear. We continued forward as best we could.

Eventually, the economic ill was transformed into political fever.

III

The gravest problem of all was the rebirth of the Red movement in Guatemala.

On November 10, 1957, when we were in the second electoral campaign, *The New York Times* commented, in an article by Paul Kennedy, entitled "Guatemala Reds Coming Home," that large numbers of Communists had been seen in Guatemala, and some were even seen in the National Palace. The Communists were named in the article. The writer then said:

"There is little doubt that Arbenz elements in Mexico were instigating and financing anti-administration groups, particularly among students, during the Castillo Armas administration. In April, 1956, the anti-Communist Guatemala Union Council charged Arbenz elements were infiltrating labor movements." The article gave the names of three known Communist leaders: Felix Valdes, Carlos Morales and Oscar del Cid.

On November 25, 1957, the *Times* again mentioned the problem of communism in Guatemala in connection with the new Partido Revolucionario. The leader of the party, Mario Mendez Montenegro, was quoted as saying: "It is only natural that returning Arbenz figures should try to infiltrate." The article then quoted another party official as saying, "We have so many Communists coming in now that we have no control." The article went on: "Miguel Ydígoras Fuentes is an old soldier in the truest tradition. While his personal and political courage are unquestioned, his grasp of modern national and international affairs are more doubtful. Mario Mendez Montenegro, in contrast, is an attorney, skilled in political intrigue, and a polished speaker. He has a long and often difficult education in plots and revolts. Basically Miguel Ydígoras Fuentes is offering a return to a strong centrist government, tolerant, but dominant. Senor Mario Mendez Montenegro is offering reactivation of the sweeping political reforms of Juan José Arévalo and taken up tentatively by Arbenz until the Communists virtually took over his program."

The chief defense against communism set up by the Castillo Armas government had been the exclusion of Communist leaders from Guatemala. This was achieved by an indirect method that favored the Castillo Armas government but not Guatemala. The 1956 Constitution contained the classic guarantee, in Article 47, that "No Guatemalan could be denied access to his land nor be exiled." The legislators added a provisional clause to the Constitution that read as follows:

Art. 6. The Executive Branch of Government is empowered to limit the guarantee contained in Article 47 of this Constitution during a period of five years (from the date of the approval of the Constitution) to the extent it may deem necessary, for the national security, with respect to Guatemalan Communists who have left the country under diplomatic asylum or because of their political activities.

The period of five years was set to expire simultaneously with the end of the term of Castillo Armas, in 1961, if he had lived. Some of the comrades did not wait for the legal period to expire and returned during the 1957 political campaign. Many of them left the country again after I had won the elections. But those who had no accounts to settle with the criminal courts returned to Guatemala when the legal period of exclusion was ended.

I have already pointed out that on the heels of the first presidential elections in 1957, the overwhelming majority I had received led my opponents to believe that I had achieved this triumph not because my own followers were so numerous, but because the Communist elements had rallied behind me. The opposition then resolved to create a party which would attract the extreme-Left and moderate-Left votes. This was done and the party was baptized the Partido Revolucionario or the Revolutionary Party.

Communists of every degree were filled with hope and enthusiasm. They must have felt like condemned men for whom prison doors open and who breathe the air of liberty after long imprisonment. They had virtually been under sentence of death for six years. They eagerly supported the new Partido Revolucionario. Their leader was Mario Mendez Montenegro.

IV

Towards the end of November, 1959, Customs Guards arrested two men on the Mexican-Guatemalan border. They were burdened down with packages of books and if they had entered Guatemala through the usual channel perhaps nothing would have been noticed. But they made themselves conspicuous by avoiding the well-marked border crossing the stations and entering Guatemala by lanes and by-paths.

Nothing alarming was found in their possession except sixty copies of a condensation of *Das Kapital* prepared by none other than the distinguished Guatemalan Communist, Victor Manuel Gutierrez. Besides the books they also bore letters, with no addresses. These missives were not in code, but written in such a manner that their meaning could be clear only to the initiated or someone in possession of antecedents.

This whole matter would be insignificant and unworthy of mention save that the letters were signed by Mario Mendez Montenegro, the leader of the Partido Revolucionario.

V

In the best "cold war" tradition, Fidel Castro sent us a wily Ambassador, Antonio Rodriguez Echazabal, with a corps of able assistants. My intelligence service immediately began to advise that propaganda, money, and instructions were being sent to the Embassy from Cuba for distribution to the underground members of the Communist Party in Guatemala. In November 1959, the Cuban Embassy extended invitations to known Communists around the world to visit Cuba.

Through our intelligence we learned that politicians, students, and others, were arriving in Cuba in ever-increasing numbers to receive military training for the purpose of forming guerrilla groups and making secret landings in Guatemala. We came to the conclusion that a concerted action was being planned, aimed at overthrowing my government. Training and funds were being made available in Cuba.

The United States' State Department evidently was becoming aware of what was going on in Cuba. On November 18, 1959, Roy R. Rubottom in a television interview declared: "The Communists of the hemisphere are receiving instructions from Moscow to frustrate and perhaps destroy the plans for the Inter-American Conference to be held in February 1960 in Ecuador." He added that "it is known that the Communists are allying themselves with anti-American nationalist groups and infiltrating and dominating labor movements. I am certain that the Communists are active in Cuba as well as in other parts of the hemisphere." He stated that 1,700 Communists were traveling between Latin America and Russia at that time, and he pointed out that this was five or six hundred more than had traveled to Moscow in 1958. He said that the Communists were spending $100 million in propaganda and other subversive plans. "Communists are penetrating in every possible part of Latin America, provoking difficulties and taking advantage of these countries."

I was glad to see that Mr. Rubottom was becoming alert to the Communist danger. Did he ever remember, I wondered, the recommendation I made in 1958 to set up a Central American front in the Caribbean?

My Ambassador to Cuba, Dr. Ricardo Quinonez Lemus, was received by the President of Cuba, Osvaldo Dorticos Terrado, in a ceremony of presentation of credentials on November 22, 1959. While on the surface my Ambassador and the

Cuban President exchanged cordial phrases of friendship, there was already a strong tension building up that was to result in the breaking off of relations within a few months.

It was not our desire, at this time, December 1959, to bring about an open schism with Cuba. We felt that the unity of the hemisphere should be maintained. Further, it was hard for us to conceive that the revolutionary government of Cuba itself would openly support subversive movements in our country. Therefore, we sent a note to the President of the Council of the Organization of American States, dated December 5, 1959, in which we briefly outlined the most salient and incriminating bits of evidence that we had gathered. We did not call for any action, nor even an investigation. One paragraph of the communication clearly expressed our sentiments at this time:

> The Government of Guatemala is confident that the Government of Cuba will understand the gravity of the action denounced and that it will at once take steps adequate to maintain peace and harmony in the continent to which we pertain.

We felt that the best method of precluding any overt action against Guatemala was to make it known that we were aware of the Communist plot and prepared to take the necessary measures to put it down. This method proved successful, for the intended military action was postponed.

Our denunciation pointed out:

1) That since May of that year (1959) we knew that a group of persons had approached Cuban statesmen, among them Raúl Castro and Ernesto Guevara, with the aim of obtaining the necessary support to carry out an armed incursion against Guatemala to overthrow the government.

2) We then said that our intelligence had informed us that aid had been forthcoming from Cuba for this subversive movement in the form of arms and money.

3) We stated that we knew that former Guatemalan President Juan José Arévalo was party to the movement.

4) We informed the OAS that some months before a detailed study that analyzed the political, social, and economic situation of Guatemala had been placed in the hands of Ernesto Guevara. The first part of the document contained a series of considerations of Marxist character. The second part was a report on the military strength of the Guatemalan military forces and their disposition in the country, and recommendations on how they could be dominated. The document reported the contacts that had been made with certain elements of the Guatemalan army and details as to the insinuations and proposals set forth. The conclusion was reached that Guatemala was the American nation where a revolution like that of Cuba could best be carried out. The amount of $50,000 was given as the amount needed to initiate the government and lay the groundwork.

We knew, and so informed the OAS, that $10,000 had been authorized by Ernesto Guevara for immediate use in the preliminary preparations and that in addition to this amount of money, military equipment and supplies were made available. These were transported to Honduras where the authorities were outwitted and the arms and supplies were landed in that country. These had been transported overland as hardware and in bales of hay. We also knew, and so informed the OAS, that Cuban guerrillas had been surreptitiously introduced into Honduras. We then let it be known that we had information regarding the training base for the would-be invaders in the Escambray Mountains in Cuba. We detailed the equipment in possession of the movement: several C-47 and Mustang planes, quantities of Springfield and Enfield rifles, bazookas and .50-calibre machine guns. There was also a Piper Apache plane at their disposition.

The Cuban representative to the OAS, Levi Marrero Artiles, declined all responsibility. He said that the charges were

totally false and that our denunciation was just one more incident in the campaign by Castro's enemies to discredit the
Cuban government. Twisting our report, with the usual in-
genuity of a sound dialectician, he told U.S. newspapers that
the equipment had "either been bought at a five- and ten-cent
store or that there was a 'financial genius' among the plotters,
who could multiply $10,000 into vast amounts."

Obviously we had neither charged the Cuban government
nor said that the equipment mentioned had been purchased
with the $10,000 authorized by Ernesto Guevara. But that
was what the United States press reported, and so, while our
denouncement fulfilled the desired end of forestalling the
event, we came out the losers in the propaganda field, because
the Cubans, by momentarily ceasing activity, refuted our
charges.

The Cuban magazine, *Bohemia,* in its December 15, 1959,
issue, came out with an acid attack on Guatemala and myself.
We were accused of propagating lies and of being tools of the
United Fruit Company. This was their old battle-cry against
Yankee imperialism. Here for the first time *we* were publicly
accused of preparing an invasion against Cuba!

Very soon we began to receive reports from South America,
from Uruguay, where former President Arbenz had taken up
residence, that recruiting of a "foreign legion" to attack Guatemala was taking place. The plot was thickening.

VI

While we continued to forestall Communist military action
against us, we could not keep the ill-intentioned money from
coming to Guatemala. The "Society of Friends of Cuba,"
which had sprung up in Guatemala soon after Castro's victory, became inordinately active. The correspondence with
Cuba became so voluminous as to come to the attention of the
postal authorities, who in turn informed me. The correspondence, which in part was turned over to us by disloyal "friends
of Cuba," who showed themselves to be better "friends of

Guatemala," revealed that a new plan for inciting, demonstrations, strikes, riots and public disorder was being plotted.

We also knew that certain members of this group had been invited to visit Cuba. Ostensibly on a mission of good will, but we were certain the intention was to coordinate plans and receive funds. The Cuban Ambassador was in close contact with the group and delegates were to be chosen. The delegates were to be the "spokesmen" for our country! Such extraordinary activities on the part of an ambassador of a "neighbor" country served to reinforce our opinion of the Castro regime.

So insistent was the Cuban clamor about an invasion being prepared in Guatemala to overthrow Fidel Castro, that on December 31, 1959, we were obliged to issue a bulletin denying the rumor.

Raúl Roa, the Cuban Foreign Minister, sent us the usual New Year's cablegram exchanged by all friendly governments.

5

THEY
TRY ME OUT
FOR SIZE

I

I REMEMBER clearly the night of July 21, 1959. We had sat down to dinner a little past our usual hour and at ten o'clock we were still conversing over coffee. At that moment we heard a muffled explosion in the distance. We immediately perked up our ears and I motioned to an aide to investigate. A few moments later there was another explosion.

We got up from the table and I went to my office. In my life there is no dividing line between business and private life. My work takes up all my waking hours and often I dream about it at night. Very shortly the report was in. The first bomb had exploded before the doors of the Palace of the Archbishop of Guatemala. The second before the doors of the United States Embassy. Anti-American and anti-Church: they could only be Communists!

The United States Embassy is across the street from the American Club and behind the Main Post Office. When I arrived to inspect the damage a great crowd had gathered. The door was protected by a metal curtain: the damage was negligible. It was the same at the Palace of the Archbishop. Tension ran high, the Minister of Defense, the Director General of Police, the Chiefs of Staff of the Army, and several ministers presented themselves at my offices. The bombing could be the signal for the offensive we expected. All departments for maintenance of order were alerted and we discussed the matter.

When I look back I am a little surprised that we took those first two bombs so seriously. These were to be followed by hundreds over a period of years. But this first terroristic act, fruitless as it was, had deep significance. It was a declaration of war.

I offered a reward of $1,000 for information as to the authors of the terrorist act.

The bombings continued. On the 26th of July at 2:30 in the morning a bomb exploded before the National Federation for Defense Against Communism. The bomb was sufficiently powerful to destroy a large window in the front of the building and to break all the windows in a school that was across the street. This was followed by a bomb on the next day, July 27, before the Electoral Tribunal. These bombings coincided with Castro celebrations.

We now had something of a pattern: Church, U.S. Embassy, anti-Communist league and Electoral Tribunal. If there was a message to be read into the pattern it was certainly of opposition to the capitalist system.

We had nine bombs in August. Most of them seemed to have been placed haphazardly, in the streets, before empty warehouses, at the Olympic Stadium. The only one that had any direct political significance was one placed near the automobile of the Minister of Foreign Relations.

This terrorist tactic was nothing new. It had been practiced in Havana and Cienfuegos fifteen years earlier. It had been suffered by Rio de Janeiro, Lima, Tegucigalpa and Buenos Aires. It was not a domestic and localized thing. The end sought was not only the material damage. Subversive propaganda was added to the acts of violence, all aimed at undermining the confidence of the people in the government.

We made a few arrests, but the organization of the enemy was too good. It followed the cell pattern. The actual perpetrators of the attempts had little or no idea who was behind them.

On the 29th of August the Minister of the Interior was summoned to Congress and questioned on the matter of the bombs. His replies to the inquiries just about sums up the whole story at that time and at the present:

"Regarding the search for and apprehending of terrorists I am pleased to inform you that we have made a few arrests. Some of these have been on suspicion and in other cases we have captured the culprits with the bombs in their hands. Nevertheless, in the courts charged with carrying out the investigations and into whose custody the prisoners are delivered, the Honorable Judges immediately set the suspects free because they find the case without merit. If no other excuse can be found, the suspect is released because his fault falls under the jurisdiction of military law and he is a civilian. In all cases where arrests were made we have been unable to obtain any convictions. It would seem that the courts are more inclined to favor the terrorists than the public."

He pointed out that the budget for the national police had not been increased in fifteen years. There was no hope that in the present situation we could obtain more money. The city had grown enormously and the number of officers was hardly sufficient.

However, we did take certain steps. To take better advantage of the existing number of police officers we withdrew all agents that had been serving as guards for private homes, offices and courts. We shut down the tailor shop and the carpenter shop in the police barracks and transferred it to the penitentiary. Thus, without affecting the budget, we were able to increase the number of men on active duty.

We also took a step that was challenged by Congress: we authorized the establishment of private police, both rural and urban, to function under the direction of the national police. Nothing like this had ever existed in Guatemala; but many private institutions were glad to pay the salaries of agents to protect their property. The result was that buildings and farms were under constant vigilance, despite the inability of the government, because of the lack of funds, to provide the service.

Early in September we caught one man in the act of placing a bomb in a public place. The army judge advocate immediately initiated a process against him and he was consigned to the civil courts. There was no legal ground for the military courts to detain him, nor even provision for a place of detainment. Within hours the justice of the peace had set him free, even while the army judge advocate was preparing the case. This was maddening. All I could do was to complain to the Supreme Court. I sent them a telegram informing them of the case and published it in the newspapers.

On that same day, September 9, we had our first nearfatality. A bomb was placed in a moving picture theatre. The newsreel was depicting the marriage of young Rockefeller to his Swedish Cinderella when a deafening explosion took place within the Capitol Theatre. Fortunately the criminal did not explode the bomb among the audience, but placed it in the men's rest room. Mario Spillari Alvarado suffered head wounds and had to be hospitalized.

These days tried my patience and more than once I was urged to take drastic measures: to impose martial law, to disband Congress, to rule by decree. It seemed to me that this was precisely what my enemies expected me to do: to flout democratic principles and to set myself up as a dictator.

II

While we had made a series of arrests, none of the individuals taken were of much importance. It was not until October that two terrorists fell into our hands who were sufficiently informed to allow the many pieces of the jigsaw puzzle to fall into place. The declarations of David Pinto Recinos and Miguel Angel Landverry (who made the mistake

of exploding a bomb along a country road in the Department
of Chiquimula on the road to the Sanctuary of Esquipulas
where a much-revered image of Christ is worshipped by pil-
grims from all over Central America) served not only to il-
luminate us as to the local culprits but gave us a lead that
went far beyond our borders. They confessed that they were
members of the Partido Revolucionario.

The type of equipment they used, the methods and even
their excuses, led us to link them to two Americans who had
been arrested during the previous month of May and who
had enjoyed the hospitality of our penitentiary since that time.
These had been caught wandering in the hills of Malacatan,
on the Mexican border, undocumented and with no proof of
legal entry into Guatemala. Further, they had explosives in
their possession, and a careful search of the countryside where
they were captured revealed an even greater cache. One of
these men was a deserter from the United States Army. He
passed himself off as Otto Born Korzeng Carodran. Why he
chose such an elaborate alias is beyond us, but then he was
only twenty-one. His assumed name was famous because it
belonged to the Nazi officer who distinguished himself by
releasing Benito Mussolini from the custody of the Italians who
had him prisoner. Even today I am not certain what their true
identities were. But they confessed that they had been paid
to come to Guatemala for two purposes: terrorism and assassination. I was to be the victim of both their activities. From
the moment I had been informed of the arrest of these men
grave suspicions had stirred in my mind. One of them had
in his possession a United States Army demolition manual
and the other still wore his army shirt. Obviously, they were
not sent by the U.S. Army. I had allowed them to stay in jail
until such time as other developments might make them important.

This came with the arrest of the two men in the Department of Chiquimula. The matter was too serious to be brushed
aside. At that time the United States was represented in

Guatemala by Mr. Lester Mallory. This gentleman so identified himself with our aims and purposes that when he left, the inhabitants of a housing project he had personally supported and watched grow brick by brick, named a square after him. I placed the entire matter before the Ambassador. I informed him of the visit I had received from the lawyers in Washington, of their threats, of the two Americans I had in the penitentiary, and of their declarations, of the rise of the Partido Revolucionario, and of my suspicions and the grounds for them. Under his further prompting I identified the firm of lawyers. He told me that there was no need for me to make any settlement with them. As a matter of fact, he said, they were gangsters and blackmailers. He offered to take the matter up with Washington and to investigate.

I then summoned the correspondent of *The New York Times,* Paul Kennedy, who lives in Mexico, to Guatemala. He came and I gave him an "exclusive." I told him very frankly that I believed there were persons highly placed in the United States government connected with the bombings. I said that I would give them two weeks for the bombings to stop, and that if the bombings continued, I would publish a list of the names of those persons.

Mr. Kennedy wrote an article that was published in *The New York Times* on October 24, 1959.

III

The bombings stopped for a while. With this turn of events I ordered that the two Americans be turned over to the United States Embassy. I saw no reason to create an international incident. They were taken from Guatemala by a special plane.

The last incident in this chain of events was a well-planned attempt to assassinate me. An American, whose name we shall not reveal, but whom we shall call Jules Potter for want of a better one, appeared in Guatemala around this time and took up residence in our most expensive hotel, the Guatemala-Biltmore. He was to all intents and purposes a banker looking for investments, and in the atmosphere of the expensive hotel he soon made friends among the diplomats and businessmen who frequented it.

Slowly the word of his activities began to filter to me. He had made a great show of going to the branch of the Bank of America in Guatemala City with a cable from Tangiers, or some place in Africa, and asking if $500,000 had been transferred to Guatemala for his account. It was not accidental that two influential Guatemalan businessmen went with him to the bank. The clerk took the cable and disappeared into the manager's office, and inside of a few moments the manager himself appeared, saying, that indeed, they had received word from Morocco, that certain funds would be, in the near future, transferred to him, Jules Potter.

This was enough for the businessmen, and for a number of Guatemalan congressmen and other officers, who had been inveigled into serving him in one way or another with offers of administrative posts in new industries he was to found, at extremely handsome and attractive salaries.

No matter how wily Mr. Potter may have been he made a mistake when he approached Dr. Felix Webster McBride, an archaeologist and explorer, who had been in and around Central America for thirty years or more and who was known to be close to me. Dr. McBride was in Guatemala establishing a new industry and Potter influenced Dr. McBride's partner into introducing them. I later learned that the first interview went something more or less like this.

Mr. Potter solemnly told Dr. McBride that he was the only man who could free his country, the United States, from a terrible menace, namely, myself. He then laid his plan before Dr. McBride who was to use his friendship to obtain an audience in the National Palace, and then to kidnap me at gun's point, and to spirit me off to the airport, after obliging me to order my aides to leave us alone. If this failed, then I was to be shot.

I really don't know what would have happened if Dr. Mc-
Bride had been intimidated into carrying out his part of the
plot. I only know that it would have been quite a scandal, because the whole thing was entirely preposterous. I could suggest a dozen better ways of doing away with me.

Fortunately, Dr. McBride immediately flew to Washington
and put the matter before the proper authorities and informed
me of the plot by letter. I sent two detectives to the Guatemala-Biltmore and they found enough evidence in his possession to arrest Mr. Potter on the spot. Subsequent information
revealed that he was indeed a very distinguished embezzler
and con man.

I turned him over to the United States Embassy and never
saw him again.

IV

In August of 1959 the foreign ministers of the hemisphere
met at Santiago de Chile for the Fifth Consultative Meeting,
ostensibly to reaffirm the principles of representative democracy and to condemn dictatorships.

The problem of the Caribbean was already very much in
the air. Not a few of us were having trouble at home.

Christian Herter, then Secretary of State of the United
States, spoke prophetically and enunciated the preoccupations
of the men of the hemisphere at that meeting. He said that
disruption of the friendly relations between any American
States would have repercussions in the entire American community. That any undermining of confidence in the efficiency
of the means and principles of inter-American tradition was
a threat to the life of the Organization of American States. He
said that the Organization was a bastion of liberty in the
world and that it was threatened by the aggressive and im-
perialistic designs of international communism. He urged the
maintenance of a strong inter-American system as a necessary
factor in maintaining the unity of America and of preserving

our liberty. He pointed out that there was great ferment in the Caribbean and suggested that a special body be set up, similar to the Inter-American Peace Board, to deal with the problem of communism.

The meeting was distinguished by the clashes between the Dominican Republic and Cuba. The Minister of Foreign Relations of the Dominican Republic placed the blame for tension in the Caribbean on Cuba, and Cuba for its part denounced the organization of a foreign legion to invade Cuba. These were very colorful exchanges, though relatively useless as neither side enlisted our sympathies.

The meeting condemned intervention in the affairs of other countries and established a Special Commission to Study Tensions in the Caribbean.

It was significant that Cuba subscribed to the Declaration of Santiago, which resulted from this meeting, and which said:

1. The governments of the American Republics should be the result of free elections.

2. Perpetuation in power, or the exercise of power without a fixed term and with the manifest end of perpetuation, is incompatible with the effective exercise of democracy.

Yet on May 1, 1960, the Prime Minister of Cuba declared: "Our enemies . . . our detractors, ask for elections . . . Some Latin American chief executives have even recently declared that the only states that should be admitted to the Organization of American States should be those that result from the electoral process . . . As if the only democratic method of achieving power was through the electoral process."

V

Communists became bolder and bolder as the months passed. I was often counseled to abandon my "soft" stand, which was nothing more than respect for the Constitution and observance of democratic principles.

One of the weapons in the hands of our enemies were precisely the liberties I insisted must continue to prevail. In September of 1959 we were confronted with the Communist indoctrination of school teachers. Towards the end of September an attempt was made to instigate a strike in the public schools as a protest over the alleged kidnapping of a secondary school teacher. In the atmosphere of conspiracy and bombings and the general tension created by growing unemployment and the constant word of mouth propaganda that was impossible to combat, the newspapers reported the disappearance of Professor Manuel Antonio Mejía Díaz, a teacher at the Belen School, the nation's central normal school for girls.

The first accusations were directed at the government. We were held responsible for his disappearance, although there could be no logical reason for our persecuting an unimportant school teacher and raising him to nation-wide notoriety. The hue and cry was fearful. We issued a bulletin denying any part in the matter and to further satisfy the demands of the press we ordered that any accredited newspaperman was to be allowed to freely inspect any houses of detention in the country, and to question freely all and any authority or prisoner whom they pleased.

Two days after his disappearance Professor Mejía Díaz miraculously reappeared and without concretely accusing anyone he requested that he be given police protection.

It so happened that the moment chosen for this incident had been the period for examinations and instead of backing the subversive movement, the students had protested bitterly against any strike that would interrupt their studies and delay the examinations. Parent-teacher organizations joined in the protests. Further, the laws of the country prohibited strikes on the part of public employees. The leftist FUMN teachers' organization had been active in attempting to foment the strike. They regularly resorted to violence, force and coercion in their attempts to paralyze the educational system.

For my part, Díaz' vague and poorly coordinated story, that he had been overpowered by unknown persons when he was on his way home from his duties, failed to convince me. I felt that the whole thing was a comedy, played to provide an excuse for a strike whose ends could only be political. It was my impression that Mejía Díaz had been hidden by his own companions, the FUMN, who were attempting to foment the strike, and intended to use him as a symbol.

Ridiculous as it may seem, while enjoying the protection of special agents that we had placed at his side—at his own request—Mejía Díaz sought political asylum in the Cuban Embassy. This naturally gave away the whole scheme. He was afraid that the true story of his escapade would come out and that he would suffer the consequences. It was only natural that he should seek the protection of those who seemed to be his best friends and most able protectors: the Cubans.

It was not long before our Department of Investigation discovered that he had made a trip on a public conveyance from Guatemala City to Quezaltenango, during the very days that he was supposed to have been kidnapped. We made this known and the entire plot was exposed.

While the idea behind the whole matter—an attempt to embarrass the government—was sound, it was carried out with stupidity and clumsiness. We were heartened in our evaluation of the hidden enemy: he could be no stronger than his agents.

VI

In January of 1960 a minor labor grievance was fanned into a national emergency that paralyzed the country for several days. The most extraordinary aspect of this assault was its lack of legal basis. The labor union within the National Social Security Institute declared a strike protesting the cancellation of special working hours—a single shift from seven A.M. to two P.M.—that had been permitted to ease transportation problems for the employees while a new building was being erected and headquarters were in a remote part of the city.

It is impossible to say whether the entire process was planned, or if the movement was merely taken advantage of by the Communists once it was under way.

As a result, all the opposition to my government rallied to support the strikers and soon the initial issue—the working hours—was forgotten and only the political issue—enmity to my government—was pursued.

The university students took the leadership of the movement and followed instructions of the underground Communist Party. An unsuccessful attempt was made to create a general strike.

Days of uncertainty and suspense ensued. The subversive opposition received money from outside of the country and this was used to buy support. I was patient and firm and ultimately the strikers ceded. They agreed to return to work and to observe normal working hours. All of Guatemala had suffered a severe setback. A handful of leftist students and Communist leaders had been able to use a labor conflict to paralyze the country. The incident achieved sufficient importance to be reported by the international press. The image of Guatemala reflected in the exterior began to be that of a struggle-torn country ruled by an iron-handed soldier.

6

I BREAK WITH CUBA

I

THE Havana newspaper *El Mundo* had a front page story on January 3, 1960, that interested me very much. It informed its readers—me, among them, although the newspaper had reached me tardily and by devious routes—that "prominent and influential Guatemalans have arrived in Cuba to visit Fidel Castro and bear with them a message from the people of Guatemala."

The prominent and influential Guatemalans were two well known leftists: Fernando Arce Behrens and Alejandro Silva Falla. The latter, Silva Falla, had a distinguished record as an agitator among the rural workers of Guatemala under Jacobo Arbenz.

Both were members of the aggressive splinter group of the Partido Revolucionario, the PUR (Partido de Unificacion Revolucionario), made up of the most radical elements. The newspaper report said in part:

"Fernando Arce Behrens and Alejandro Silva Falla arrived from Guatemala as envoys of the Society of Friends of the Cuban Revolution. The most distinguished intellectual figures

in Guatemala make up the board of directors . . . [it then
named several known Guatemalan Communists] . . . They
have come to deliver a message of solidarity with the democratic plans of the Cuban government to Commandant Fidel
Castro. 'The government of Guatemala, but not its people,'
said Silva Falla, a former Congressman and Director of the
National Peasants' Federation [during the Arbenz' regime]
'seems to ignore that in our country there is a large group of
Cubans who were obliged to go into exile because of their
crimes and depredations during the Batista government, and
who openly conspire against Cuba. These criminals are allowed to maintain radio programs to attack the revolution; to
install camps to train mercenaries that are financed and paid
by Batista, Trujillo and representatives of the powerful im-
perialistic interests of the United States. The people of Guatemala also aspire to live in liberty, independence and under
a humane government [such as that of Fidel Castro!]. They
are closely identified with Cuba and with its revolution which
is a voice that has inspired America.' "

In the interview, Silva Falla boasted that he had gone to
see his "good friend," "Che" Guevara, with whom he had
shared diplomatic asylum in the Argentine Embassy in Guatemala. "When Arbenz fell, he went to Mexico and I to Argentina. I can assure you that no matter who may invade Cuba,
there are many Guatemalans who will rise up and come here
to defend the Cuban Revolution."

Silva Falla also accused my government of carrying out
fraudulent elections, and limiting suffrage. He said, "those
electoral manipulations will cause blood to flow." Regarding
his presence in Cuba, he said:

"We do not care if on our return to Guatemala we are
arrested and imprisoned. Our mission is to deliver to Commandant Fidel Castro, to Fidel, as you call him, the message
sent to him by the Association of Friends of the Revolution
of the Cuban People. We want to establish cultural exchanges
with Cuba, and social, political and student exchanges."

He was asked about the Agrarian Reform in Guatemala. (We had continued to give lands to the *campesinos,* under the programs dating from the Communist governments. However, the Communists had given land to the *campesinos,* in mere tenure, in line with their rejection of private ownership; we were extending full deed and title.)

"Yes, we find the agrarian reform in Cuba quite just. [Although Castro was following the Communist policy of giving land only in tenure.] This should be done in Guatemala, where more than 75 per cent of the population is rural. The *campesinos* must be armed, to be able to defend the land they receive. This [the Cuban revolution] is a true revolution, we hope it does not suffer the same fate as ours [the pro-Communist regime in Guatemala under Arbenz] where traitors and counter-revolutionaries destroyed it."

II

On the 12th of January, I instructed my Minister of Foreign Affairs to have a little talk with the Cuban Ambassador. We had learned many interesting things about his interest in our economic and political life.

The conversation between Ambassador Antonio Rodriguez Echazabal of Cuba and Dr. Jésus Unda Murillo, our Foreign Minister, was recorded in an Aide Memoire. This document was later submitted to the Organization of American States in a formal denunciation of Cuban intromission in Guatemala, dated November 15, 1960. It is therefore a matter of record. I quote briefly from this Aide Memoire, as follows:

"The Foreign Minister advised the Ambassador of Cuba, acting on instructions from the President of the Republic, that he had confidential information that elements contrary to the government were recruiting men and training them for an invasion of Guatemala, with the help of certain Cuban officials.

"The Ambassador replied that surely the information was incorrect, but that at any rate he would write to his Chancellery informing them.

"The Foreign Minister then advised the Ambassador that persons connected with the Embassy of Cuba in Guatemala were distributing propaganda, money and other political means to opposition political parties in Guatemala, as well as to labor union movements and enemies of the government, and that this without a doubt was intromission by Cuban diplomats in the internal affairs of Guatemala. The Ambassador replied that this could not be, but that he would investigate . . ."

III

The rising temperature of agitation everywhere in Latin America made it obvious that Guatemala was not an isolated victim. Certainly what was happening in Guatemala—rising revolutionary parties, strikes, Cuban intervention, subversive activities—was but part of a hemisphere-wide plan.

Each day in Guatemala the ties between disaffected persons, Communists, opportunists, and the Cuban Embassy became closer and closer. The opposition leftist parties became bolder and bolder in speech and action. On the 28th of January the Public Relations Secretary of the PUR made a statement that was published in the local papers saying that the country was in danger of a civil war. He went as far as to say that the commencement of hostilities was imminent. On the same day the Partido Revolucionario called for a general strike. Three Cuban intelligence agents arrived in Guatemala by air from Mexico on January 27. They were received by well-known Guatemalan Communists. The visitors were Manuel Nieto F., Afortunato Estefano and Guillermo Prieto. They were received by Francisco Villagran Kramer, Mario René Chavez, Francisco Ponce, Luis F. Balcarcel and Edmundo Guerra Teinheimer.

A member of the Cuban Embassy, José Luis Valdez Marti,* who had been retired from the delegation when he was implicated in whiskey smuggling, re-entered Guatemala from Honduras with a diplomatic passport. The Cuban Ambassador attempted to cover up the fact that his government continued to protect Valdez by telling us a complicated story about lost passports. We had to accept his explanation but the man was again forced to leave the country. There is no doubt he was an intelligence agent.

Meanwhile, it was rumored in Cuba that I had made a special trip to the impenetrable jungles of Peten, accompanied by the United States Ambassador, to inspect the location of a secret airstrip to be used to bomb Cuba. Forty-eight hours after I had discussed this matter it was announced by Radio Havana. Only three persons had known of the conversation: a member of the United States Embassy, a retired army colonel who held a high post in the administration of the Peten region, and myself. There is no doubt that it was the second party who revealed our conversation.

I later learned that a clandestine short-wave radio transmitter was operating in Guatemala City and communicating with a contact in Honduras. This last was more powerful and communicated with Cuba. This was the system over which messages were sent and received. The retired army colonel dedicated himself to subversive activities and was removed from his high post.

President Eisenhower issued a statement on January 26, 1960, in which he said: "The United States Government views with increasing concern the tendency of spokesmen of

*This man later returned to Guatemala in the role of an anti-Castro exile and in time headed the Revolutionary Council. I was obliged to deport him in December of 1962 for unscrupulous activities. He found asylum in Honduras, and from the capital of that country, Tegucigalpa, promptly denounced me as having been handsomely paid for allowing bases in Guatemala to be used to attack Castro. He did me more honor than harm by also falsely stating that I had been offered $1,000,000 to recognize a Cuban government in exile. There is no doubt in my mind that he was a Castro agent.

the Cuban Government, including Prime Minister Castro, to create the illusion of aggressive acts and conspiratorial activities aimed at the Cuban Government, and attributed to United States officials or agencies." He also said that it was regretted that efforts over the past year to create a basis for understanding and confidence had not been reciprocated by the Cuban government. We had had no such illusions, but we were glad to see the United States coming out openly against the Cuban conspirators.

Shortly thereafter, General C. P. Cabell, Deputy Director of the C.I.A., declared before the Subcommittee of the Committee on the Judiciary of the United States Senate, investigating Communist infiltration in Latin America, that Communist activity in Latin America was "more intense" than in the Near East or North Africa. He pointed out that the Communist program in Latin America included using the Cuban Revolution as an example of the "wars of liberation," whose success should be imitated by all anti-imperialists in Latin America. The strategy of the supposed "liberation movements" was to use non-Communist nationalists and intellectuals, and groups of youths and students, for their ends. "The training of Latin American leaders by the Communist Party of the Soviet Union has been continuous since 1953 and it was stepped up considerably in 1956. Since 1956, the Communist Party of China has also been indoctrinating and training Latin Americans," General Cabell declared. We were aware of this, and soon saw on our own soil the tangible results of the assiduous program of undermining democratic institutions by persons trained in both Russia and China.

Intermittently we suffered spurts of subversive activity. They were poorly timed and fruitless. On February 4, 1960, telephone lines were cut in the eastern provinces of Guatemala. These apparently unconnected incidents—sabotage in one part of the country; caches of arms in another; Guatemalans making violent statements in Cuba; a consistent campaign to undermine the confidence of the people in the government in the local newspapers; opposition congressmen placing every possible obstacle before progressive legislation in Congress— all led us to believe that a concerted action was being prepared. We suspected that the Partido Revolucionario, together with other disgruntled political groups, was working with money that was being received from outside of Guatemala, principally Cuba. And as ever—the terrorist campaigns of night bombings. In the first months of 1960 the bombs became more powerful. They were placed in private automobiles and in public buses. There were some bodily injuries, but as yet no deaths.

IV

His Excellency, the Cuban Ambassador, had a private secretary named Victor Alberto Mirabal Acebal. No attempt had been made to accredit this individual as a member of the Embassy staff. He had been expelled from Honduras and accused by that Government of being a blackmailer and a subversive. He attempted no blackmail in Guatemala but he did pursue an active life inciting subversion, directing the placing of terrorist bombs, and conspiring with the disaffected nationalist groups. He was the Ambassador's right hand man in subversive activities.

On the 8th of February, at eleven o'clock in the morning, the Ambassador of Cuba was again summoned to the office of the Minister of Foreign Relations. Dr. Unda Murillo bluntly told the Cuban Ambassador that his private secretary was active in internal politics in Guatemala, that he had attended political meetings, and even secret ones. That he was constantly in the company of persons known to be disaffected to the government. He told the Ambassador that he knew that this person distributed propaganda, money, and instructions to labor leaders, and contributed funds to opposition political parties. He said that to the best of his understanding all these

activities took place with the full knowledge and consent of
the Ambassador of Cuba, Antonio Rodriguez Echazabal, to
whom he had the honor to address those remarks.

The Cuban blandly denied the charges. He did, however,
admit that the man was his private secretary and offered to
take steps to see that these activities ceased, if it were true
that they were going on.

Dr. Unda Murillo told me that he could barely contain
himself before the brazen attitude of the Cuban. He informed
the Ambassador that Guatemala under no circumstances could
permit foreigners to meddle in Guatemalan internal affairs and
he gave the Ambassador forty-eight hours to see that Mirabal
Acebal left Guatemala.

This shook the Cuban Ambassador. We had been so tolerant
that perhaps he believed we had no intentions of ever putting
our foot down. Still he countered, requesting four days' time
for the man to arrange his affairs and leave the country.
Surprisingly enough, and if I remember correctly against my
instructions, the Minister granted the request.

The Minister then informed the Ambassador that information continued to come from secret sources in Cuba that preparations for an invasion of Guatemala were still going on, and
that we considered the activities of Mirabal Acebal to be part
of this plot.

The Ambassador again denied the charges and came out
with the usual offer of advising his chancellery so that the
matter could be placed before his government.

The Minister informed the Ambassador that this was exactly
what he had replied on the other occasions but that no word on
these matters had ever been received by us from Havana. The
interview was closed when my Minister informed the Cuban
Ambassador that attacks on Guatemala had been appearing
with increasing frequency in the belligerent Cuban press.

The upshot of this little incident was that Mirabal Acebal
refused to leave Guatemala voluntarily. We were obliged to

order his arrest and deport him like a common criminal. We were amused that the Cuban government made no comment nor protest on his expulsion.

Mirabal Acebal, himself, however, did protest his expulsion. He prepared and distributed a mimeographed bulletin in which he candidly confessed his intervention in the internal politics of Guatemala and spewed a shower of insults on the government and myself. We allowed him to leave despite his attitude. But we asked ourselves, and our people, in a bulletin: What would Fidel Castro have done if such an incident had taken place in Cuba? Obviously the person who dared act and criticize so brazenly, could have but one fate: the wall.

V

In this climate of agitation and uncertainty we followed certain clues and they led us directly to our "old friends" who had recently been to Cuba. A conspiratorial group led by Fernando Arce Behrens and Mario René Chavez García was discovered and we sent a number of these men to the penitentiary. Behrens gave an interview to the Cuban magazine, *Bohemia,* accusing the Government of Guatemala of having given Pedro Díaz Lanz, the first Cuban of prominence to defect from the Castro regime, an airplane and bombs to attack Cuba. It will be recalled that Díaz Lanz actually confessed that he had flown over Cuba, but only admitted to dropping propaganda leaflets. Chavez García had returned from a trip to Havana with a supply of Castro insignias. He had instructions to deliver these only to "persons of extreme confidence," and to tell them to wear them surreptitiously and that they would be extremely useful "when the right time came." Of course, this meant, when *our time* to go to the wall came, which they were preparing for us, in collusion with Cuba.

Guatemalan Communist leaders returned from visits to Havana with large amounts of money to be used for subversive and terroristic activities. They had funds to purchase arms in Guatemala, to recruit guerrilla troops, and to prepare brigades to transport arms that were discharged on lonely coasts far from any inhabited regions. The entire activity was one of assiduous preparation of a strong "fifth column."

While the internal preparations in Guatemala went ahead we knew full well that the disaffected Guatemalans, who had fallen from power with the ousting of Arbenz, were in Havana, plotting. Here there existed a complete training base, with airstrip and schools. The "students" were taught details of the coastal and interior geography of Guatemala.

We issued a press bulletin on February 22 to this effect. It was our hope that the Cubans and the other persons implicated would be inclined to drop their plans when they learned we were forewarned.

Two days later, on February 24, we learned that a sloop had landed arms in the Bay of Omoa, in Honduras. Two men, Luis Manuel Zuniga and Agápito Robledo Castro, were captured, but only after they had successfully transported the weapons to an interior point. According to declarations made by the prisoners, the weapons were destined for Guatemala. Both men were of notorious Communist background. Zuniga Saravia was the son-in-law of Abel Cuenca of El Salvador who had been active in the Communist Party from the 1920's. The other was the director of an extremist newspaper published by the Honduran Communists in San Pedro Sula, *La Tribuna Revolucionaria*.

Our intelligence further informed us that a Guatemalan citizen, one José Raúl Bardales Mejía, was in the coastal town of Honduras of Puerto Cortes precisely when the sloop was discharging the cargo of arms. The arms had been landed in Honduras because I had given instructions that the Atlantic zone be closely patrolled by sea and air.

Bardeles Mejía was captured by the Honduran authorities

and declared that the movement to which he belonged was perfectly organized in cells, each made up of groups of ten or twelve men, who were stationed all along the Guatemalan-Honduran frontier. He boldly stated that they were awaiting "the right moment to throw a coordinated attack across the frontier to end the corrupt government of Miguel Ydígoras Fuentes." He also said that there was a similar organization along the Mexican-Guatemalan border which would enter into action simultaneously with the attack from Honduras.

We made all the foregoing public in a bulletin dated February 24.

After Mirabal Acebal was expelled from Guatemala, Rodriguez Echazabal, the Cuban Ambassador himself, took over the contact work with the Communists and the disaffected politicians who betrayed their country for their ambitions. By this time it was known to them that they were under surveillance so they acted with greater caution. In March the Ambassador was seen in his car, on one of the roads outside of Guatemala City, near the town of San Juan Sacatepequez, in deep conversation with a leader of the PUR party, Marco Antonio Villamar Contreras, a famous leftist. This immediately gave us something to sink our teeth into.

It was useless to undertake a legal action against the PUR. Even if we had sufficient proof of the conspiratorial nature of their meetings, we would still have a hard time in the courts, which were controlled by the opposition. I decided on a direct course of action.

I instructed the Minister of Interior, Dr. Carlos Salazar Gatica, to summon these men to his office and to place the facts before them. The leaders of the PUR party were summoned and among them were Julio Camey Herrera, Alberto Paz y Paz, Julio Valladares Castillo, Adrian Vega Ruano and Marco Antonio Villamar Contreras himself. They were confronted with the facts and told that the government knew of their connections with the Cuban Embassy, that they were implicated in the terrorist bombings. The Minister invited them to cease and desist from such activities. They of course denied everything. The press had gotten wind of the meeting and were milling in the corridors around the Minister's office. They were refused admission and told nothing. The Minister requested the politicians hold their tongues about the matter, and offered to do the same.

This, they did not do! The conspirators began to give declarations to the press the minute the meeting was over. Of course their version was twisted. They said we had threatened them! They complained that they already had one foot in jail! In other words, we were accused of doing everything we should have done but had not.

Only then did we break the story to the newspapers. The Minister held a press conference and said that the PUR had guerrillas stationed along the Honduras-Guatemala border; that the PUR was involved in a plot to overthrow the government; that if the government did not have exact and precise information at hand it would not have made it known to the public; and he pointed out that instead of inviting these men to this office and suggesting that they stop their subversive activities, they should have been arrested, and thrown in jail.

The Cuban Ambassador was not inhibited by our declarations regarding his activities. Ignoring the usual channels of diplomatic procedure, something which I often did myself, he protested certain statements of mine by issuing a bulletin to the local newspapers. Among other things he said: "Cuba is not and could never be a center for the distribution of Communist propaganda and Communist instructions; the desires of the government and people of Cuba are to maintain and extend the most cordial relations with all other countries, especially those of Guatemala and its illustrious government."

We took this with a grain of salt and my press secretary replied with a few facts:

"The President did not say that Cuba was a Communist center, despite the fact that this is daily proclaimed by the press of the entire continent, and even by the Cuban press itself . . . Who can doubt that Communist propaganda is sent from Cuba throughout the Latin American nations? This does not mean that the Cuban government is distributing it. But Cuba today has very cordial relations with international communism, as can be seen in the trips of the highest Cuban political figures to Red China, Russia, Yugoslavia and other satellite nations . . ."

Our Guatemalan Communists, who had been confined in the penitentiary for conspiring against the government on their return from Cuba, were not inactive even behind the prison walls. By the end of March we were certain that something was in the air. The first incident was a protest from Fernando Arce Behrens that he had been tortured.

The local press of course took up the refrain, and while I gladly would have given orders to wring his neck, if it had been legal, I ordered that the charges of torture and beatings be investigated. It turned out that Arce Behrens had scaled a low wall that separated two recreation yards within the penitentiary and leapt, evidently with the intention of harming himself, because his legs were bruised. It so happened that the director of the penitentiary was watching him. He then got hold of the seed of a cashew fruit, which, if rubbed on the skin on a spot that has been sucked for a few seconds, leaves a mark exactly like the contusion from a blow, and with the help of another inmate, applied this trick to himself. It perhaps seems strange that this almost childish matter should be mentioned here. However, childish as it was, it served to stir up the local papers and create a propitious atmosphere for what followed.

By the end of March 1960, we learned that the incident of the penitentiary was to be used to extend the state of uneasiness in the country. The local press carried a story that unidentified groups of "revolutionaries" were going to hold demonstrations before the penitentiary demanding that the political prisoners be released. At the same time a formal accusation against the director of the penitentiary for torturing the inmates was drawn up and presented to the courts by Eduardo Vasquez Becker, who was acting on behalf of the Law Students Association, "El Derecho." This Vasquez Becker had a record going back to 1954 of fraud and embezzlement. In 1958 he had been implicated in an organization that was printing Communist propaganda in Guatemala.

On April 22, 1960, Arce Behrens was successful in fomenting a mutiny in the penitentiary. Despite our precautions, money had been smuggled to him and he had bribed guards and other inmates. As a result tremendous activity of all political groups coincided with the uprising. We were not caught completely unaware, and the riot was put down with only one casualty, a prison guard, who was knifed.

We now saw the fruits of the Cuban investments in Guatemala. While the security of the country was not endangered, every point open to attack being alerted and securely guarded, I felt that the best way to forestall any action was to let the enemy believe that he had been betrayed on all sides and that all his plans were known. This would discourage any further moves and avoid bloodshed and violence. I ordered my press secretary to prepare a bulletin and to distribute it to all the radio stations, newspapers, and news agencies in Guatemala. I knew that it would be a matter of minutes before the bulletin was in the hands of the leader of the subversive movement. Had we known exactly who he was and where he was we would of course have proceeded to capture him. But the truth is, that at this early stage in our war with communism, we only had sketchy information. However, we issued the bulletin, dated April 22, 1960, the same day as the mutiny, which read in part:

"In the shadow of a political party of the extreme Left, an insurrection has been plotted in this country, which receives its orders from Cuba, and has a strategy copied from that of Fidel Castro in the Sierra Maestra, and which is called the '20th of October Movement.' This criminal plan, guided from Russia, implemented in Cuba, fortunately is in our hands in its entirety, thanks to the patriotism and civic pride of a people who do not support or condone traitors. The aims of these false apostles, disguised as revolutionaries, is to infiltrate and undermine the democratic institutions of Guatemala, until the government can be overthrown, and then impose a reign of terror under armed militias which would supplant the regular army and thus upset the normal life of the nation. The '20th of October Movement' is supported by funds that are supplied by 'Che' Guevara—who left unhappy memories in Guatemala—who takes the money from the Cuban National Bank or receives it from Russia."

We then outlined all we had learned regarding the organization over the previous months, how the groups were made up, where they were operating, what arms they had and we publicized our accusations against former President Juan José Arévalo and Jacobo Arbenz of collaboration in the plan.

On the following day, April 23, 1960, I sent a message to my Ambassador in Havana, Ricardo Quinonez Lemus, instructing him to return to Guatemala City for consultations. The Cuban Ambassador to Guatemala, Antonio Rodriguez Echazabal, had left the country some time during March and never returned, officially, at least. We suspected that he had returned incognito.

On April 25, 1960, I instructed my Ambassador to the OAS to file a protest and to request the simultaneous inspection of Cuban and Guatemalan territory to ascertain exactly where invasion preparations were taking place. The controlled press of Cuba had continued to attack Guatemala and we were daily accused of being an anti-Cuba base. Cuba, of course, did not consent to the inspection. Even then, she had too much to hide.

VI

More information was gathered from different sources on the subversive activities within my country. And on April 27 or 28 the Associated Press released a story which quoted Jules Dubois, a *Herald-Tribune* Latin American correspondent, and revealed accusations made by Cuban Captain Manuel Vallafane, who had defected as a Cuban military attaché in Mexico. He accused "Che" Guevara of sending men and money to Guatemala for the overthrow of my government, and of using diplomatic channels for the purpose of subversion.

We knew that the Embassy of Cuba abused the privilege of the diplomatic mail to import money and propaganda directed against our democratic institutions. We knew that subversives were financed. It was impossible to tolerate any longer the continued activity of the agents of international communism under the protection of diplomatic immunity.

For this reason, on the night of April 28, 1960, I announced over the combined radio and television networks of the nation, and to the world, that we were closing our embassy in Havana and asking the Cubans to close their embassy in Guatemala.

As a result, Cuba's Foreign Minister Raúl Roa went on the air in Cuba and directed a most insulting speech against Guatemala in which our participation in an anti-Castro movement was prophesied. At the same time, the international news agencies carried reports that former Guatemalan President Jacobo Arbenz was on his way to Cuba.

In this age of a new type of war, undeclared and invisible, Guatemala was now embarked on a war with Cuba and international communism. From that moment, not one single day was to pass that the relentless prosecution of the battle was diminished by either side.

7

THE GENESIS OF A "NATIONAL LIBERATION" MOVEMENT

I

THE fruits of the work of the Communist base in Cuba ripened and flowered in Guatemala. While the Cuban Embassy had been closed and could no longer work openly, the months in which they had pursued their ends under the cloak of diplomatic immunity had served to consolidate what is termed a "National Liberation Movement."

General C. P. Cabell, Deputy Director of the Central Intelligence Agency of the United States, made the following statement on November 5, 1959, before the Subcommittee of the Committee of the Judiciary of the United States Senate:

> The so-called national liberation strategy seeks to offset Communist numerical and political weakness through international organizational support and clandestine techniques of infiltration and coordination. The immediate objective of the strategy is to provoke political or revolutionary action by sympathetic non-Communists, but politically influential elements, for the purpose of establishing an environment within which the Communist Party is free to organize and expand. The Communists hope for the es-

116

tablishment of governments which are, at least, neutral in the EAST-WEST struggle, if not actively pro-Soviet, and which will guarantee them political opportunity equal to that enjoyed by genuine political parties. It is within such a framework that the Communists then hope to achieve the so-called peaceful transition to socialism, which will find a temporary alliance with the national bourgeoisie within a government of national unity gradually replaced by a Communist-controlled "people's democracy." The program of communism in Latin America is designed to develop unity of action around popular issues such as *antipathy to dictatorships, inflation,* a desire for greater industrialization, nationalization of resources, and wider and more stable markets. It encourages opposition to U.S. participation in regional programs affecting Latin America. *The program also involves expansion of the Communist propaganda apparatus to include a network of news correspondents who will develop support for the 'national liberation' strategy,* while discrediting free world news agencies as agencies of imperialist propaganda. The techniques of Communist action are both overt and clandestine, legal and illegal, national and international. The techniques are carried out by the national Communist parties and their fronts, with support from the "fraternal" Communist parties abroad, and the international Communist fronts. All of these operate through known Communist Party members and secret party members in nominally non-Communist organizations. Communist literature may be imported under false inventories; financing is accomplished through a great variety of channels which conceal the extent and origin of funds. Mass recruiting, as attempted several years ago, has in some cases been deemphasized, while emphasis has been given to selective recruiting of key individuals and secret members.

Here, in a nutshell, is the explanation of Communist strategy in Guatemala. It is also the story of other Latin American countries.

While the national forces that take part in these movements do not always completely accept the Communist doctrine, and often ignore that they are working hand in hand with the Communists, they are moved by a desire for change. But in the case of Guatemala the desire for change was for a transfer of power from my centrist policy. I was attempting to maintain the social advances achieved in the past, laying plans for further social progress, and trying to take anti-communism out of politics. My administration was trying to curb the aspirations of the Communists while at the same time attempting to correct evils of unequal distribution of capital and poverty by exerting pressure on the well-entrenched upper classes. When my position is considered, it is obvious why many forces were willing to support movements to eliminate me from the scene. The Right because I threatened the status quo, and the Left because they saw no hope of dominating my government.

Early in May of 1960, the Guatemalan Communists received a document from Havana dated May 2, that contained instructions from "Che" Guevara aimed at coordinating the revolutionary effort. Edmundo Guerra Telheimer, Guatemalan Communist, exhorted the revolutionary parties to organize a brigade to receive guerrilla instructions in Cuba. On the 13th of May an important member of the underground PGT announced that $75,000 had been received from Cuba via Mexico to finance subversive work and that other amounts would be received at regular intervals.

The boldness of the Communists is demonstrated in an invitation extended by the Student Council of the USSR to Leonel Roldan Salguero to attend a summer study session in the Soviet Union. The document reads:

> The Student Council of the USSR has studied your petition and has included you among those who will participate in the International Summer School that will be held this year in Crimea.

It then outlines the expenses, which ostensibly would be for the account of the student. The summer school was to be

held in early July. The document under reference was dated
April 28, 1960.

The trained investigator who headed our Department of
Special Investigations at that time, after studying the document, came to the conclusion that the invitation was a countersign wherein Roldan Salguero was advised that the USSR had
agreed to all the arrangements made by the different Communist organizations, and that in agreement with the Guatemalan center, the PGT, he was to be one of the Guatemalans
to receive Communist training in Russia.

"These invitations are only extended when the Communist
is considered of outstanding talent and after extensive investigation into his background," the chief of investigation
told me. "The invitation is signed by the secretary of the
student council, N. Diko, and it is tantamount to an entry
visa for Russia, recognized in any embassy or border station."

Roldan Salguero was a trained primary school teacher,
although he did not practice that profession. He had been one
of the agitators in a serious strike and was immediately put
under police surveillance.

II

Terrorist bombings became more frequent. We captured
suspects, the courts released them. After a long discussion
with my Ministers of the Interior and Defense we issued a
bulletin, hoping to warn the innocent. It was dated May 15,
and read:

> Since the 12th of this month we have seen a new wave of
> terrorism sweep over the country. Bombs have shattered
> homes and property. These bombs have been manufactured
> by members of the PUR (Revolutionary Union Party) and
> the PGT (underground Communist party). We know that
> members of the Liberation Party (anti-Communist) are also
> involved in this plot. We know that the organizers of this

terrorism are receiving money and explosives from Fidel Castro and that they are being coached by Cubans who are in Guatemala. Recently, a young lady was the victim of an explosion and her right arm was mangled. This was provoked by traitorous Guatemalans and undesirable foreigners.

III

On May 17th I received a special report from an international anti-Communist group. It said that Juan José Arévalo had entered into an agreement with Fidel Castro and that Jacobo Arbenz was expected to adhere, as this had been one of the Cuban's conditions for lending his aid. The plan was to overthrow my government by first creating civil commotion and instability to weaken it. This would be followed by an armed strike, either from within through an uprising of the army, or by an invasion, or both. Arbenz was to lead the armed groups and he was supposed to go to the Sierra Maestra to take command. Instead of worrying me, this news made me quite optimistic. With such a leader as Arbenz they would not go far.

My intelligence reported that several local political parties were involved, and that the divided revolutionary movement had united under this banner. I was informed that members of different splinter factions of the subversive Left had met on May 4 with PGT leaders. During the meeting they were addressed by Carlos Leonidas Acevedo who told them that a meeting between Juan José Arévalo and the Cubans had taken place in Maracay-Caracas (where Arévalo lived) and that the following had resulted:

1) Arévalo had the financial backing of Fidel Castro, and we have reason to believe that part of the money was to be used to translate into English and publish in the United States his book, *The Shark and the Sardines,* in an attempt to influence liberals in the United States in his favor. The Cubans had made it a condition that Jacobo Arbenz participate.

This was because he had close ties with international communism dating from his rule in Guatemala, which had been strengthened by his trips behind the Iron Curtain after his downfall and his constant contact with Moscow during his exile in Uruguay.

2) It was believed that Juan José Arévalo could not be denied admission to Guatemala; and, since it was impossible to achieve a victory by civic means, they would take recourse to violence. It was expected that the presence of Arévalo at the time of an armed coup would be decisive.

3) It was decided that immediate action was to be taken in Guatemala to consolidate the opposition and to create a group to agitate, hold demonstrations, and harass the government. It was known that caches of arms had already been prepared in Guatemala and that one cache was in the Cuban region.

The chief of intelligence warned me that the organization of labor unions was going ahead so rapidly and with such success that we could expect an outburst at any moment. It was impossible to foresee what labor group would take the lead, or where the violence would erupt. But he was certain that this well-planned movement would begin with some labor problem, grow into a national crisis, find support in all the extremist political parties and among the university students, and at the height of the agitation, after the country had been disorganized by strikes, the military strike would come.

I ordered that all of this information be made public, and my press secretary prepared a bulletin which was released on the following day and published in the Guatemalan newspapers on May 19, 1960.

On the 20th, it was confirmed that Jacobo Arbenz had arrived at Havana from Uruguay. He was immediately received by Prime Minister Fidel Castro and taken to the Sierra of Escambray by Raúl Castro, head of the Cuban Armed Forces, to visit the training camps where the legions were being prepared for the strike against Guatemala.

Arbenz was preceded to Cuba by José Manuel Fortuny, who had been his chief counselor during the height of the Communist control of Guatemala.

IV

The arrival of Arbenz in Cuba coincided with extraordinary activity among the different subversive groups in Guatemala. We alerted all our forces and doubled our coastal patrols.

Such agitation had a depressing effect on business. It was reported in the international press, and bets again were placed on how long I would last. The opposition took this opportunity to accuse the government of being responsible for the unhappy economic situation in the country.

Things went well for the Communists. They got the ear of such heterogeneous groups as the Christian Democrats, who should have, because of their philosophy, given the subversives a wide berth. But this was not the case, and we saw the Communists gaining ground. We knew that many were convinced my days were numbered. It was said that our government was inept, that it was ruining the economy of the country and becoming dictatorial. People are always anxious to place the blame for poverty on someone. It was easy to blame the government, despite our untiring efforts to balance the budget. Meanwhile, those congressmen who belabored the government were at the same time placing obstacles before legislation that would alleviate the situation. I had plenty to worry about. Indeed, these days of 1960 were the darkest of my life.

The interference of Cuba in the internal affairs of other nations was notorious, and evident for all to see. It was natural that those who were receiving money from Cuba should dedicate themselves to criticizing my government and doing everything possible to create an atmosphere propitious to their plans. We did all we could to warn the people of Guatemala of what was happening, but the only effect was to have our warnings ridiculed as "pipe dreams" and "scares" intended to create exactly such a situation as the Communists wanted, so that we could "transform our democracy into a dictatorship." If I had wanted to, all of the democratic institutions of Guatemala could have been abolished overnight; I had sufficient cause to declare a national emergency and to rule by decree until the last subversive had been exiled or jailed. However, I did not do this. It would have been only a palliative, it would not have remedied the fundamental situation. (It was then that I coined the phrase: *"mientras Guatemala goza la democracia, yo la padezco,"* which, translated, means that while Guatemala enjoyed democracy, I suffered it.) Besides, such iron-handed action was precisely what my enemies, and the enemies of democracies, were waiting for. There was no path but Christian resignation and faith in the people of Guatemala.

V

An alarming symptom of what we could expect appeared on June 1, 1960. Marco Antonio Villamar Contreras, who had already been to Cuba, and who was closely identified with past Communist regimes, had the effrontery to use a local radio station to call on the people of Guatemala to support Fidel Castro and to incite them to open rebellion.

He not only insulted me and the government in the grossest terms, but he made it clear that he had the support of forces alien to Guatemala and that these were ready and prepared to support organized terrorism.

Arbenz returned to Montevideo, Uruguay, on June 2, 1960. His return coincided with the visit of Cuban President Dorticos to that city and they conferred for over half an hour in the Hotel Victoria. They conferred again that night. When Dorticos' activities with local labor groups and Peronist leaders became too flagrant and were protested, he hastily abandoned Uruguay.

The vanguard of the Russian "diplomatic corps" in Havana arrived almost at the same time that Dorticos returned. There were only ten in the first group. However, there were already hundreds in Havana. We knew this for a fact.

We had information that the powerful teachers' union, the FUMN, and the school children's association, the FUEGO, were to be the lance-head for the prepared movement. They went on strike.

On the night of June 10 a bomb exploded in Guatemala City, and two Molotov cocktail-bottles of varsol with fuses were found in two neighborhood theatres during the evening performances. Luckily, our informers had advised us and the bombs were found before they exploded. Later, at ten o'clock, a bomb exploded in the street.

This Communist "call to arms" failed because two of the bombs were found in time and the one that did explode was inconsequential.

Meanwhile the teachers' strike prospered. The two "front" student and teacher organizations were themselves only tools for the leftist politicians who in turn were tools for the international Communist movement working through Cuba. Despite our efforts to appease these two front organizations, nothing availed. There was no possible benefit for the students in supporting the strike and most of them had no conception of what was going on. They were fed explosive ideas by companions who were no more than paid agitators, and school after school fell into the grip of the unseen organization.

The FUMN or the teachers' front could by no stretch of the imagination represent the interests of the students. It had received instructions from the "Friends of the Cuban Revolution." It did not even represent the bulk of the teachers. In our present circumstances, when we were having difficulty meeting current commitments, and had been advised by the International Monetary Fund to reduce our expenditures, most of the teachers had resigned themselves to accepting a scale of pay in relation to the rest of the country. But a small group had formed to keep the cause of higher salaries alive, and this was the FUMN. But it did not represent the thousands of teachers all over the country. Yet, it had called the strike against the government and because of its infiltration of all the ranks, and control over the students achieved by paid agitators, it succeeded in paralyzing our school system.

The FUMN was actively supported by the FUEGO, the student organization. Nothing could be more ridiculous than an organization of primary and high school students militating in a political movement that concerned them not at all. The FUEGO did not represent the students as a whole either if it can be considered that children between six and eighteen should be represented in a political organization.

On the 14th of June we were met with street incidents, students began to create disorders in forms that could only be called acts of juvenile delinquency. Three students of a vocational school were picked up by the police when they dedicated themselves to stoning a national monument. The amount of damage they achieved was of course minimal, but they managed to injure a lady who was passing by. We knew exactly what was behind the incident but all we could do was take the boys to their parents and ask that discipline be applied at home.

VI

Guatemala, like all other countries, is receptive to rumors, and the weapon of the whispering campaign was constantly used with success. A baseless rumor that I was to take a mysterious voyage and deposit the presidency began to circulate. It began with a little item in a local paper that hinted that a "high official of the government was planning an overland trip to the United States." It was described as a "publicity stunt" and my well-wishers lamented that such a thing be undertaken when the country was in a state of crisis. The whispering campaign then said that I was suffering from an incurable disease. The local papers also commented on this and touchingly reported "the long faces" of the senators when they heard the "sad news." Then it was rumored that I was going to ask for four months' leave of absence for a trip to England. In a few days it was official. A radio commentator said that I had sent an official communication to Congress requesting that the First Presidential Designate (corresponding to the United States' Vice President) be sworn in.

At this point I chose to make a personal appearance on the television circuit. I categorically denied that I was contemplating any pleasure trips, that all could see that I was in good health and needed no "rest cure." Here is exactly what I said:

"Those who have Castro's money in their hands should not be too confident that the government can be overthrown. Nor should anyone believe what is said by the partial national press intent on stirring up strife. I do not blame the students. I have always respected them. I have never used students as fronts in my political campaigns, not even when I was in open opposition to the government. But we all know that this is an old trick in Guatemala, dating back many generations, often used to remove some public official from office."

If the use of student fronts was an old stratagem, it had been highly refined by the scientific application of the Pavlov principles by the Communists. Youngsters were given small amounts of money, and these were steadily increased until, like addicts, they had to have more and more. And, since the work asked of them made them leaders among their fellows, and distinguished them, the students followed the Left like sheep.

VII

The teachers' and students' strike took on a new, but not unexpected, turn. Since the government had ceded on every demand made to it, hoping to delay the outburst, the strikers were told to make a demand that could not be conceded by the government, for both legal and economic reasons. In other words: they wanted to avoid a settlement at all costs. It was demanded that the teachers' seniority register be reinstated, and that wages be scaled according to its provisions.

This in itself was sufficient proof of what was behind the movement. As President of the Republic, I could not revive the register; it was a matter solely for Congress, even if it were economically possible, which it was not. However, the entire movement was directed against the executive branch. In a country where the democratic processes are used and not abused, the matter would have been taken care of by petitions to congressmen. But in Guatemala, this was not conceivable. What made the matter even more ridiculous was that Congress would not respond to my entreaties to consider legislation on matters of prime interest to the nation and which would go a long way towards solving our social and political problems, such as the Income Tax Law, the bi-lateral agreement with the United States for guaranteeing loans, and the Civil Service Law, all of which had been tabled under the protest of being "studied" for months and years. Much less heed would Congress give me, if I were to propose such a thing as the reinstatement of the teachers' register, which would have been fatal to our economy.

A newspaperwoman who had never been very friendly toward my government, Irma Flaquer, made a patriotic gesture early in June when her column in a local newspaper aptly entitled, "What Others Cover Up," denounced a subversive meeting between representatives of the FUMN and leftist leaders, Guillermo Toriello, who had been Arbenz' Ambassador to the United States and a rabid leftist, Colonel Carlos Paz Tejada, who had been the leading Red in the Arbenz army, and others. She said they had formed a close alliance with the FUMN, offering Lord knows what rewards for its support, and their plan to overthrow the government was based on having the present agitation as the cornerstone of the movement. They went so far as to appoint the triumvirate that was to succeed me after I had been "removed" from office: Colonels Enrique Close de Leon, Ernesto Paiz, and Carlos Paz Tejada. Despite these denunciations there was little we could do.

The FUMN and its representative among the students, the FUEGO, began to apply pressure on primary school teachers. This was denounced to the government on July 1 by groups of parents, who appealed to the government to intervene. The method used was to threaten the teachers with physical punishment unless they stayed home and at the same time to scatter false rumors regarding the closing of schools. When the teachers did not go to their work because of the threat of violence and children found their school closed and heard that the school was on strike, it was more than natural that they should return to their games. This then was a victory, because the school was "on strike" and inoperative. This tactic was skillfully applied throughout the nation and to the uninformed observer, influenced by the denunciations of the government in the newspapers and radio, it seemed as if Armageddon had come.

In high circles we too feared that it had come, but we faced the situation courageously, placing more emphasis on avoiding mistakes than in aggressively disrupting the process of agitation. If at that moment we had resorted to wholesale violence, or if I had lost my head, I can, in all honesty, state that I would not be telling this story. Fortunately, the police and army maintained the most stringent discipline, and despite insults, threats, and even violence, they stood their ground impassively. The most we did was to break up street demonstrations with tear bombs. Violence would only have created more violence.

It was heartening to have at least one group of students come out and publicly denounce the manipulations of the leftists. The unaffiliated students of the Faculty of Economic and Social Sciences addressed a message to me, on July 12, signed by Gilberto Secaira, wherein they made it clear that they were not supporting the strike of the FUMN and FUEGO. The message read as follows:

"Non-political students of the Faculty of Economics advise that they have categorically refused to support the strike declared by the Association of University Students. The strike was approved at a meeting attended by only forty-three persons, including fourteen members of the FUMN who have nothing to do with the Faculty of Economics. Eighty-five per cent of the students of this faculty are non-political, and we do not support the subversive movement of the FUMN and FUEGO, or Marxists, although the board of directors of the students' association, which is controlled by Reds, may spread rumors to the contrary."

This was indeed the crux of the situation. A handful of Communists controlling an entire organization because the bulk of the membership did not want to be entangled.

The problem of education is of course a vital one for my country and one of my chief preoccupations was to see that it was not too adversely affected by the loss of public revenue. We maintained all the existing services the best we could, but if we acceded to the demands of the strikers it would mean an increase of $3.9 million per year which would slowly increase into an astronomical amount. We brought this to the attention of the strike leaders but to no avail. Their response was to launch a renewed attack on the government, and obeying instructions from their friends, bitter reproaches were directed at the armed forces. These were subjected to every kind of insult and attack.

It may be asked why recourse to legal measures was not taken. The fact was that we had no legal recourse. The libel laws did not contain provision beyond guaranteeing opportunity for refuting in the same medium that printed material which the court found to be libelous. All we could do was reply as logically as possible, but logic was fruitless amidst such dissension and chaos. We could have applied the criminal law to them, but this I would not permit.

Congress was in recess but the standing committee was

meeting and it was pressed by the strikers to convoke a special
session to consider the demands. The president of the legislative body said in relation to this, "I feel completely supported
by the Constitution. Congress should be free to legislate without pressure from minorities. This is the basis of representative government. We cannot convene Congress because there
is nothing concrete to consider. The problem of the teachers'
register and increasing wage scale would have to be studied by
the Committee on Education and, until their investigations
were returned with their recommendations, Congress would
have nothing to discuss. Further, this problem cannot be
separated from the general problems of the country. We now
have under consideration a project for a civil service law which
will definitely separate the public administration from politics. In this way all government employees will be protected."

The newly appointed Minister of Education, Professor Gus-
tavo Argueta, a man brought up from the ranks, had the following to say:

"We have bent over backwards to keep the teachers at work.
Their first demands were not related to the wage increase.
The whole thing started with a complaint against the principal
of a school. We fired the principal and the [then] Minister
[of Education] resigned. I have replaced the principal, but
only Congress can reform the laws of the country."

Many teachers wanted the schools to open, but the strike
leaders would not allow them to do so, resorting to violence.
A spokesman for the strikers denied they were on strike: "We
are not on strike," he said. "We have only stopped working.
This is a national emergency and Congress should convene to
solve our problems."

We allowed the striking teachers and students to hold a
mass meeting in the Central Plaza. I believed it best to let
them give vent to their ire, in words, at least. And this
would also reveal to all who listened exactly what their ends
were. A moderate-sized crowd attended and all the speeches
were of an eminently political nature. One young man, who

had not even started to shave, was reported to have said: "We want to build a true democracy in this country, to change the word 'democracy' from a meaningless piece of demagogy in the mouths of those who are defrauding the national interests." I asked myself exactly what kind of democracy it was the young man asked for. The democracy of Hungary, under the machine guns of the Russians? Or perhaps the democracy of Castro, that had subjugated the universities and the educational system to a mere means of indoctrination? Didn't the young man realize that the very fact that he was permitted to address a public meeting was the essence of democracy? That democracy could not work miracles, such as were needed to concede the demands of the strikers, but had to face the hard reality of the economic possibilities of a nation?

One student, who was later to travel to Cuba as a reward for his "brilliant intervention," was reported as saying: "Now is the time to act! We must clench our fists and seek justice with our knuckles." A man who spoke for an unidentified labor group said: "Committees have now been formed throughout the country for the paralyzation of the entire life of the nation in a general strike!"

In this labyrinth of forces it was hard to know just who was acting on orders from the central organization of the movement and who was acting on the inspiration of the moment, or perhaps inspiration from a bottle. It is difficult to believe, but the leaders of the FUMN actually sent a cablegram to the Organization of American States protesting that freedom of expression was suppressed in Guatemala. They had the opportunity of making this known to their followers in the newspapers that sympathized with them, over the radio stations under their control, and before mass meetings. While they cheered Fidel Castro and Khrushchev with impunity, and slandered the government, and disrupted the studies of the children of Guatemala, they had the opportunity of making it known to the world that freedom of expression was suppressed in Guatemala!

On the 18th of July, while the country was in the grip of the most violent agitation, when every school was closed, when the streets were the scene of disturbances, when the spirit of every Guatemalan was perturbed, the opposing factions made a grave mistake. They paid a man to take a live hand grenade into a neighborhood theatre, during the afternoon performance, when it was filled with children, women, and idlers. At five minutes past five o'clock the hand grenade shattered the interior of the theatre. It killed one man instantly, Martin José Argueta Sierra, whom we suspected became a victim of his own felonious deed. Thirty-two others were wounded, many of them seriously. Two men, a woman and a child, died in the hospital. Children between the ages of seven and sixteen were wounded. Here is a partial list of the victims with their names:

Ovidio Alfonso Delgado, seven years old

Enrique Garcia, sixteen years old

Sonia Yolanda Alvarado, thirteen years old

Clara Luz Obregon, fifteen years old

Nelly Sak, fourteen years old

Eduardo Rosales, thirteen years old

Alvaro Rosales, ten years old

Gloria Elizabeth Catalan, eleven years old

Gloria Rosales, ten years old

Ofira Delgado, eleven years old

Marta Alicia Alvarez, twelve years old

Leonel Alvarez, eleven years old

Rosalvina Argueta, nine years old

Miguel Alvarez, eleven years old

Enrique Lopez, 16, and Alicia de Samayoa, an adult, died in the hospital, a few hours later.

It is impossible to describe the scene. I visited the theatre a few hours after the attack; the floor was still stained with blood and the seats were twisted and shattered.

When the Minister of Defense held a press conference that night and announced that martial law was being decreed and constitutional guarantees were being suspended, one of the newspapermen said: "This is one time when the people of Guatemala welcome martial law and the suspension of guarantees."

Throughout the agitation the legal status of the nation had remained unchanged, every citizen had recourse to all his democratic rights. But when those rights were abused to bring death to innocent children in an attempt to incite the people, it was time to check political activities in every way possible.

The teachers' strike collapsed like a deflated balloon. Whatever sympathy the public may have had with the movement— and I know it did not look on it with too friendly eyes—was dissipated in the terrorist action. "Why do they attack children?" people asked themselves. I knew to what depths political ambitions and fanaticism could drive men. Here was tangible proof. It was sad and heart-breaking to visit the little victims where they had been hospitalized. We cared for them as best we could, but lost limbs could not be replaced, scars could not be erased from young faces, and the dead could not be brought back to life.

Even then the subversive movement did not admit defeat. Schools all over the country renewed their work, demands were forgotten, and messages of solidarity were sent to the government; but attempts were made to create new incidents and mobs of ruffians, each villain paid a few pesos, milled in the streets shouting insults at the military patrols. They defied the curfew and did everything they could to provoke authorities to violence, but they were unsuccessful. They even went so far as to fire on the police from roofs and doorways, but the police did not fire back. A bomb exploded in the Main Post Office Building, two employees were wounded. Handbills continued to circulate and we knew that as long as there was money in the treasury of the subversives the disturbances would continue.

VIII

The Associated Press commented on July 22, 1960, that the disturbances in Guatemala had coincided with the visit of Jacobo Arbenz to Cuba. It also mentioned that Karen Khatchatarov, press attaché of the Soviet Legation in Uruguay, had traveled to Cuba, to coordinate the agitation in the Caribbean Zone. The Soviet press attaché had been made an honorary member of the "Friends of the Cuban Revolution," in Uruguay, a few days before his trip to Havana. Colonel Jacobo Arbenz was reported to be an adviser of the association.

Our own Embassy in Uruguay sent a report stating that Fidel Castro was certain that I would be deposed, and that was why he had called Arbenz to Cuba.

We obtained conclusive proof of the participation of the Cubans in the strike and subsequent agitation when a letter written by a group of labor and union leaders and the Director of the Agrarian Reform Bureau of Cuba, Antonio Nunez Jiminez, to Marco Antonio Villamar Contreras, fell into the hands of our intelligence. It needs no comment.

Havana, June 15, 1960

Senor Marco Antonio Villamar Contreras
Caribbean Plan, Guatemala

. . . persons of trust, and of unlimited authority, who were responsible for achieving and maintaining power in Cuba, and whose experience should be used to advantage in Guatemala, advise as follows:

a) Surprising popularity for the Communist aims among the working masses;

b) The difference between the other parties and the official aims of the reactionaries who want to form one single united front;

c) Frank and decisive action by the Communist leaders in the creation of closely united cells; and,

d) Total resistance by the Communists of any official provocation.

In this way Guatemala will be given a brilliant opportunity of succeeding, with our moral and economic assistance, and of thus creating a popular republic in Central America, which will serve as a bridge for our world battle to enter Central America and as a base in which to train local Communists for subversive work in the other Central American republics.

Consolidation of our ranks should be the watchword of the Communist Party. This will serve to maintain most of our forces intact. In addition, each one must use his time to best advantage in training the working masses to prepare them to carry out the missions that will be entrusted to them by the Communist Party. These movements will be well organized and ostensibly inspired and directed by nationalist leaders who are notoriously democratic and vociferously anti-American, but ready for battle.

Our companion, Francisco Martin, chief of the Bureau of the Union for the Assistance of the Latin American Democracies, admitted that he was greatly alarmed because of the lag between the issuing of instructions and the implementation of Communist activities in Central America, which were prescribed during the last conferences which were attended by our most trusted delegates from the Communist parties of America. Martin said, "In line with the present situation in Guatemala, the companion leaders of the party activities have, during the past two months, received four separate and very clear instructives, calling for extreme caution, because the public actions are being denounced by the government as subversive and as the work of the enemies of the masses of workers seeking the abolition of public power and the present government."

The first step in this important plan is the inciting of high school teachers and students. We are advised by our companion, Lorentzen, that unfortunately the university students have become reactionary and that we cannot count on them; but, on the other hand, he says that he has precise information that the youngsters of junior high school and post-primary age are malleable material in the hands of their professors. We have sent you sufficient funds for this work with our companion, Rachel.

The Communist activities through the CARIBBEAN AGENCY remind you, above all, of the preparations that are being made to put in operation the CARIBBEAN PLAN for Central America, which is supported by Communist elements and others, which will also further the Soviet penetration in Latin America.

There is no doubt that the situation created in Guatemala is watched with great interest by the CENTRAL BUREAU FOR THE ASSISTANCE OF DEMOCRACIES IN LATIN AMERICA, and that is why our organizations can be greatly favored as indicated in the studies and instructions sent to you through our cell in El Salvador (Roque Dalton) so that the errors of 1954 will not be repeated.

With a brotherly greeting for our Guatemalan companions, we desire they meet with success.

UNITY IN DEFENSE OF THE COUNTRY, THE WORKING CLASSES AND OF OUR CONQUESTS AND OUR ORGANIZATIONS.

DEATH TO THE CLERICAL-EMPLOYERS IMPERIALIST REACTION.

CUBA: A SPUR IN THE BATTLE FOR LATIN AMERICA.

signed by: Antonio Nunez Jiminez, Dwelling Union; Marcelino Fenandez, Sugar Union; Carlos Mas Martin, Agricultural Union; Vicentina Antuna, Cultural Union; Candelaria Rodriguez, Chief of the Office of National Defense.

IX

At this time, another even more extraordinary letter came to light. It was found when the meeting place of the conspira-

The Indian population of San Mateo Ixtatan captured seven of the ten insurgents and the other three were soon trapped . . . If the army contingents had not arrived soon after, it is likely that they would have been massacred by the indignant natives (Page 213).

Thus, Francisco Barrios de Leon, (left) "student leader," who was in reality a Communist agent, served to expose the connection between the supposedly "nationalist" movement in Guatemala and international communism (Page 212).

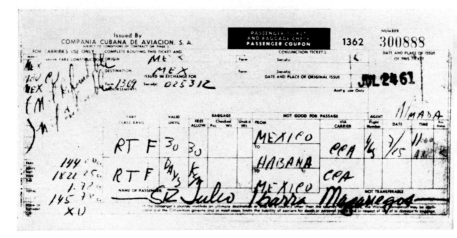

Travel documents and ticket issued to student leader Julio Ibarra Mazar-riegos (Page 221).

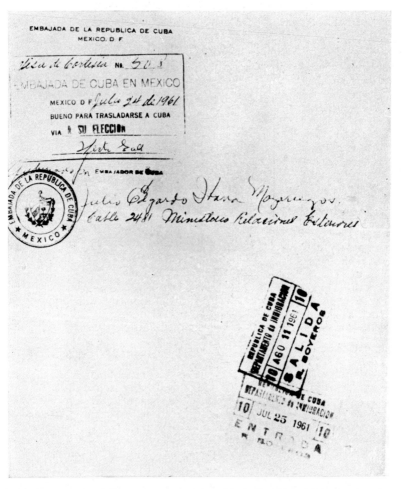

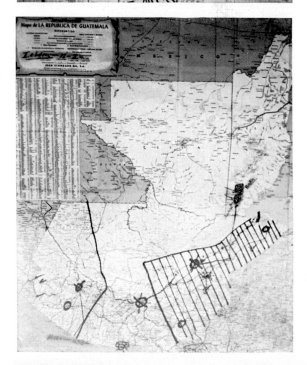

In the lining of his suitcase were found two military maps, one of Guatemala and the other of Guatemala City. These were carefully annotated and contained the military strategy intended to coincide with the political agitation that was being planned for six months later (Page 212).

FESTIVAL MUNDIAL

HELSINKI 1962

It is said that the Soviet invested $104,000,000 in transportation and expenses to carry thousands of students from all over the world to Helsinki (Page 221).

Another significant symptom of the intervention of International Communism in Guatemala was the attendance of Guatemalan students at the Eighth Helsinki World Youth Festival which was sponsored by the Kremlin (Page 220).

As the reader can see from copies of Airline Passenger Manifests . . . literally hordes of youngsters from all the countries of Latin America . . . were transported . . . to Cuba (Page 221). The manifests clearly state that the transportation is "courtesy" or free, and many of these are for account of the ICAP (Cuban Institute for Friendship of Peoples) (Page 221).

A shower of bullets and rockets fell at the very door of my office (Page 226).

I took up a light machine gun . . . and followed by my close aides, I went out into the street to take personal command of the Presidential Guard of Honor, three blocks from my residence (Page 226).

Two (defecting) aviators arrived in a jeep . . . Instead of meeting . . . the Commander of the Guard of Honor . . . they came face to face with the President himself (Page 227).

COMMUNIST THREAT TO THE UNITED STATES THROUGH THE CARIBBEAN

HEARINGS

BEFORE THE

SUBCOMMITTEE TO INVESTIGATE THE ADMINISTRATION OF THE INTERNAL SECURITY ACT AND OTHER INTERNAL SECURITY LAWS

OF THE

COMMITTEE ON THE JUDICIARY

UNITED STATES SENATE

EIGHTY-SIXTH CONGRESS

SECOND SESSION

PART 9

AUGUST 27, 30, 1960

Printed for the use of the Committee on the Judiciary

UNITED STATES
GOVERNMENT PRINTING OFFICE
WASHINGTON : 1960

82540 O

It is also that, upon instructions, I spent 2 hours and 35 minutes on December 17, 1958, with Batista, and I told him that the United States or rather certain influential people in the United States believed that he could no longer maintain effective control in Cuba, and that they believed it would avoid a great deal of further bloodshed if he were to retire.

Senator EASTLAND. That was on instructions of the State Department?

Mr. SMITH. An ambassador never would have a conversation like that, sir, unless it was on instructions of the State Department.

Senator EASTLAND. Let me ask you this question. As a matter of fact, isn't it your judgment that the State Department of the United States is primarily responsible for bringing Castro to power in Cuba?

Mr. SMITH. No, sir, I can't say that the State Department in itself is primarily responsible. The State Department played a large part in bringing Castro to power. The press, other Government agencies, Members of Congress are responsible.

Senator EASTLAND. Would you say that the American Government then, including all of its agencies, was largely responsible for bringing Castro to power?

Mr. SMITH. The American Government, yes, sir, and the people in the American Government.

Senator EASTLAND. Yes.

Mr. SMITH. We refused to sell arms to a friendly government, and we persuaded other friendly governments not to sell arms to Cuba.

Yet on the other hand revolutionary sympathizers were delivering arms, bodies and ammunition daily from the United States. We were lax in enforcing our neutrality laws.

Senator EASTLAND. To Castro.

Mr. SMITH. Yes, sir, to revolutionaries under Castro.

Senator EASTLAND. You had been warning the State Department that Castro was a Marxist?

Mr. SMITH. Yes, sir.

Senator EASTLAND. And yet in spite of that, of your advices to our Government, you say that our Government was primarily responsible in bringing Castro to power.

Mr. SMITH. That is absolutely correct.

Senator DODD. May I ask a question? Did you ever discuss Castro with Mr. Rubottom?

Mr. SMITH. Yes, on numerous occasions.

Senator DODD. Can you tell us what his attitude was toward Castro?

Mr. SMITH. In all due justice to Roy Rubottom, I think that Roy Rubottom was under terrific pressure from segments of the press, from certain Members of Congress, from the avalanche of Castro sympathizers and revolutionary sympathizers who daily descended upon the State Department, also their official representative, Betancourt, and Rubottom may have taken the line of least resistance.

From personal experience I have learned that many very influential sources in the United States are dedicated to the overthrow of all dictatorships. They are as opposed to anti-Communist rightest dictators, who are friendly to the United States, as to the Communist dictators whom they regard as progressive. They adopt a doctrinaire attitude toward this question which is so impractical that they ultimately unwittingly defeat themselves. If dictatorship versus democracy were the only question that faced us, it would not be difficult to make a decision. However, as we are in the midst of a struggle for survival, other considerations are pertinent.

Mr. Earl E. T. Smith, at that time United States Ambassador to Cuba, appeared before the Committee on the Judiciary of the U. S. Senate on August 27 and 30, 1960 (Page 14).

tors was searched. It was in very bad condition and had evidently been carried in some secret pocket and been read by many. It showed clearly that Fidel Castro and his followers, and especially "Che" Guevara, were disillusioned by the leaders of the different Guatemalan political parties who had collaborated with them, and with the underground PGT, because the greater part of the funds that had been sent to them, had been stolen, and because they realized that they had been deceived when they were told that my government had no popular support.

The document reads in part:

> You should no longer use the teachers for purposes of agitation because the money that was sent to them, in large part, disappeared without producing any tangible or practical results. We must insist that popular movements be organized, even if the million dollars that have been offered have to be used. New tactics should be observed, and one of these is to organize shock brigades. This should be easy with the recent unification of the revolutionary forces. This work should best be given to the Communist Party; we suggest that the movements be organized as follows: in the Department of Guatemala, Francisco Corado, member of the PGT and Director of the FASGUA; Joaquin Maldonado, member of the PGT and secretary of the FASGUA; Roman Santos, member of the PGT and secretary of the Union of Motorists; Miguel Valdez Giron, member of the PGT and a Director of the FASGUA; Moises Quilo, member of the PGT and Director of the FASGUA; Tranquilino Lopez, coordinator of the Central Committee of the PGT and elected to membership in the Central Committee of the III Communist Congress recently held in secret in Guatemala. For the Department of Esquintla, Mario Arévalo, professor and member of the PGT; Department of Quezaltenango, Dr. Saul Osorio Paz, member of the PGT. Do all you can to find companions you can trust in the other departments.
>
> Leave the leadership of the movement in the hands of Dr. Mario Mendez Montenegro, Colonel Carlos Paz Tejada and

Dr. Francisco Villagran Kramer, since each feels himself to be presidential material, they will not hesitate to carry matters to extremes.

The following men should be kept in second rank: Julio Valladares Castillo, Otto Palma Figueroa, Hector Morgan Garcia, Carlos Leonidas Acevado, Julio Camey Herrera and Julio Gomez Padilla, as well as Humberto Gonzalez Juarez and Colonel Adolfo Garcia Montenegro.

Economic support will continue to reach you and you will be able to count on popular adherence to the movement, but the movement should be of a purely nationalist color.

We hope that as soon as the state of siege is lifted, you will commence with street demonstrations. If you follow the instructions we have sent you, it is certain that the government will be overthrown. Use as a slogan for your popular demonstrations: "The drastic measures which the Government has loosed against the people."

Keep in contact and be united with the groups around Ortiz Passarelli and Dr. Cordova Cerna, because until we are able to overthrow Ydígoras they represent valuable allies and should not be despised; once the objective is achieved they will of necessity pass into the ranks of the followers of Ydígoras and the liberationist files.

You should act with vigor and serenity at this time. We cannot allow you a new defeat such as you suffered in the teachers' movement, which was based on your false belief that Ydígoras had no popular support. It is now evident that you must act with the support of only minorities; therefore, these should be made up of trained and disciplined revolutionaries. Once the internal movement is under way—which must not fail, under your responsibility—help will reach you from abroad.

(signed) *CHE*

8

INTERNATIONAL
COMMUNISM
MUSTERS ITS FORCES

I

THE close ties between the Guatemalan Communists and the Cuban government were proclaimed for all the world to see. The importance of *association* in the Communist frame of reference will not escape anyone, and the presence of Jacobo Arbenz on the platform at Las Mercedes on July 26, 1960, when Fidel Castro celebrated the seventh anniversary of his revolution, was no mere accident. Arbenz sat between a high member of the Red Chinese government and a diplomat from behind the Iron Curtain.

The presence of Arbenz in Cuba served to inspire the extremists in Guatemala. With hard cash in their hands, instructions in their heads, and murder in their hearts, they saw the presence of Arbenz in Cuba as symbolic that the enormous strength of the Communist world was behind them. We were informed that Juan José Arévalo had sent a personal message to our revolutionary friend, Colonel Carlos Paz Tejada, that he would soon receive a large amount of money, and the same report said that Arbenz was smuggling arms into Guatemala.

On August 4, 1960, just to keep the record straight, we

filed a protest with the Inter-American Peace Board about the "illegitimate interventionism" the Cuban government was perpetrating in Guatemala. Our ambassador in Washington, Carlos Alejos, informed the commission as follows:

> For the moment, I will limit myself to informing your Excellency that the Government of Guatemala has information that has been fully confirmed that the sloop, *Theresa*, sailed from Cuba with a cargo of arms, that it arrived at a place called Barra Colorado on the Atlantic coast of Costa Rica where it took on board persons of different nationalities, including Cubans, and sailed on the 3rd of August for Guatemala with manifestly aggressive ends.

The inhabitants of our Pacific Coast region were surprised when a strong searchlight played on the dark beaches in the middle of the night of the 30th of July. It was identified as coming from an unidentified submarine. The submarine was sighted twice and duly reported to the Defense Department. Air patrols were sent out but were unable to contact the craft.

II

We had a lot of trouble closing up our Embassy in Havana and it was not until August 12, 1960, that the last employees arrived in Guatemala. The two men, Mr. Augusto Ruano Moreno and Carlos Humberto Cajas, who had been left in charge of the Embassy, sounded like fugitives from behind the Iron Curtain. Ruano Moreno had been chargé d'affaires when relations were suspended on April 26, and he told me that the Embassy had been watched day and night by the Cuban police and militia. They had stopped every person who entered or left the Embassy and questioned them.

They were particularly interested in keeping anyone from seeking asylum in our Embassy; and Ruano Moreno told me that he was awakened by shots at two o'clock one morning and later found out that two men had been killed and several taken prisoner when a group tried to reach the Embassy seeking asylum. They felt that their lives were threatened every moment and they stayed as close to the Embassy as possible. According to Ruano Moreno they were practically in a state of siege and had difficulty in obtaining food.

When relations were suspended with Cuba there were six refugees under the protection of the Embassy. The chargé d'affaires immediately requested safe-conducts for these persons and the Cuban Foreign Minister, Raúl Roa, extended them. However, only two persons were allowed to leave Cuba under the protection of Guatemala. The other four safe-conducts evidently were canceled. They were able to get the two men out of Cuba with the help of the Costa Rican Embassy; and when they took these men to the airport they were roundly insulted by the people in the streets and at the airport. There was a fantastic display of arms, machine guns, grenades and pistols.

In short, the whole panorama was disastrous. Ruano Moreno told me that at length when he saw that it was impossible to obtain safe-conducts for the remaining four men, he advised the Cuban Foreign Minister that he was going to transfer them to the Costa Rican Embassy, because the Guatemalan Embassy had to be closed. Since the consultative meeting of the Foreign Ministers of American States was to meet in San José, Costa Rica very soon, the Cubans finally extended the safe-conducts; and after much difficulty the men were finally allowed to leave. The Cubans had finally relented because they did not want the incident to come up at the meeting.

These and many other things were learned from these two victims. Ruano Moreno spoke of the presence of Arbenz in Cuba. He said that he had seen Arbenz on television and heard him say that his government had been a failure and that his failure was the direct result of his having failed to destroy the Guatemalan Army, which had betrayed him. He then said that Arbenz had promised to return to Guatemala, where the people awaited him and that then he would destroy the army and create a national militia.

Events continued at this accelerated pace. Late in July

a large group of guerrillas were reported in the village of Maquelizo, Department of Santa Barbara, in Honduras. Three of the men had identification cards signed by the leader of the Partido Revolucionario, Mario Mendez Montenegro.

Twenty-five thousand handbills attacking my government were printed in Honduras and distributed in the banana regions. We also learned that the sloop *Theresa* was owned by Raúl Pineda, of La Ceiba, Honduras, and that it had sailed for Bluefields, Nicaragua en route to Corozal and Zambo Creek in Belize and the Guatemalan coast.

Francisco Rios, a Communist, declared that the Guatemalan situation "would be cleared up very soon." He said that a hired assassin had been commissioned to murder me. He also spoke of a plot against the President of the Honduras. We had received information from Europe about the recruiting of men in Yugoslavia, and this word from Honduras served to confirm the news. We informed the government of Honduras of our findings.

The emergency which had been created by the teachers' and students' strike continued, tension was high in Guatemala, and the air was filled with every kind of rumor. After consulting with my ministers we decided not to suspend martial law, as the initial period of thirty days had expired, but to extend it for an equal period. This measure restricted to a certain extent the conspiratorial and terrorist activities.

III

The Sixth and Seventh Consultative Meetings of the Foreign Ministers of the Organization of American States met in San José, Costa Rica, between August 13 and 30. The first meeting was called to consider the denunciations of Venezuela against the Dominican Republic for the attempted assassination of President Romulo Betancourt. The meeting censured the Dominican Republic and speeded the downfall of the Trujillos.

The second meeting, or Seventh Consultative Meeting, was called to consider the Communist threat to the American continent. I sent a large mission to Costa Rica under the leadership of Foreign Minister Unda Murillo. While the climate of the meeting was totally adverse to the Communist government of Castro, the agenda of the meeting, which could not be disregarded, had been drawn up in general terms to consider the Communist infiltration in the hemisphere. Guatemala was the only delegation that pointed its finger directly at Cuba, and, while Cuba refused to sign the resolution condemning the Communist infiltration of the hemisphere, and calling for measures to combat it, no direct action against Cuba was taken.

At the outset of the meeting, we were under the impression that the seventh meeting would take up the case of Cuba, and we were determined that a resolution against Cuba be taken. We did all we could to influence the meeting in this respect but as no specific accusations against Cuba had been included on the agenda the meeting did not develop in this direction. But I insisted that our position be made perfectly clear and instructed the Foreign Minister to speak out loud and clear and condemn Cuba in one of his addresses. If we had been able to obtain a resolution condemning Cuba at that time, August 1960, the entire history of the Western Hemisphere might have been changed.

When an agenda is drawn up for a meeting, it must be rigorously observed and any speaker who dares to mention matters that have not been previously approved for discussion, leaves himself open to being called to order by the chair. Nevertheless, I instructed Foreign Minister Unda Murillo to disregard this state of affairs, and with full authorization and support of the government, he made the following statements before the Seventh Consultative Meeting of American States:

"During the last year, international tensions in the Caribbean have profoundly concerned the American governments . . . The government of my country . . . has expressed its firm desire to maintain friendly relations with all nations but much to our dismay, shortly after the initiation of the present government of Cuba, and when we expected that relations between Guatemala and Cuba would be bettered, or at least maintained within the traditional cordiality that has always existed between our two countries, unfortunately, this was not the case, and on the contrary, our relations deteriorated. Cuban diplomats in Guatemala approached groups of known Communists in Guatemala that were plotting a chain of conspiratorial and disruptive activities, while subversive movements against my country were plotted in Cuba by Communists and pro-Communists. These circumstances obliged us to present a protest to the Council of the Organization of American States on December 6, 1959, to make this known to all the nations of the continent.

"Why, it can be asked, do hostile acts against Guatemala originate in Cuba? Why is Guatemala a special target for Communist conspiracies, the American people can ask? Why is Cuba pointed to as the source from which these acts originate, directly or indirectly, that have brought on a state of tension, not only between the two countries, but also throughout the Caribbean area, where both Cuba and Guatemala occupy important positions? The answer to these questions can only be found in the fact that Guatemala was once within the Soviet orbit when the governments that tainted the democratic principles of the revolution of October 1944 attempted to channel the social and political development according to alien precepts foreign to American norms, with the objective of creating a state on the Marxist pattern, subject to the tutelage of international communism. The Soviet Union saw its aims frustrated in 1954, and since its prestige as a great power suffered, it has sought the path to retrieve its position of 1954, and it found a good instrument in the illusions planted in the minds of certain leaders of the Cuban revolution, that they must fulfill a mission of redemption. A program that is stimulated by the presence in Cuba of Marxist agents who, with reproachable ends, unwilling to accept the lesson of the repudiation they suffered, attempt to reconquer the power they lost six years ago.

"It has been possible to see that important positions within the Cuban government have been taken over by international communism, which lends credence to the belief that this is the first step taken to project Communist dominion over other countries of America, with the decided support of the Soviet Union.

"Early this year the intervention of the Cuban diplomatic representatives on the one hand, and the subversive activities originating in Cuba, were so flagrant that on several occasions the Cuban Ambassador was summoned to the Ministry of Foreign Relations and informed that the situation was becoming intolerable.

"The warnings . . . were fruitless and the situation deteriorated until we saw ourselves in the difficult position of being obliged to withdraw our diplomatic mission from Cuba.

"If we look at this matter from a continental point of view, the Government of Guatemala has been gravely concerned by the ill-intentioned policy of the Soviet Union, that has been pursued by some members of the Cuban government in recent times, because this could be the beginning of greater intervention of Communist imperialism in inter-American affairs, aimed at the subjugation of other nations of this hemisphere.

"Our country recently suffered a series of civil commotions as a result of agitation carried on by a small group of persons trained in the methods of international communism . . . The unfriendly acts of the Cuban government towards Guatemala culminated in an official invitation presented by that government to former President Jacobo Arbenz, to take part in the celebrations held on July 26 of this year. He occupied an important place on the presidium and alternated with the Cuban and Communist leaders in making use of the official tribunal, amid the applause and cheers of the leaders of the Cuban revolution, to threaten the constitutional government of Guatemala. Arbenz, as all know, had carried Guatemala into the

Soviet orbit, but he was overthrown by the national movement of 1954; he abandoned the asylum that had been generously accorded him by another country, and took up residence in Cuba to intensify the subversive campaign against Guatemala which is being carried on to this very moment.

(deleted material)

"Guatemala firmly maintains that the interference of the Soviet Union in the affairs of this hemisphere coupled with threats of armed aggression, and the rapid extension of its policy in this continent, using the Cuban regime as a channel, constitutes an act of flagrant intervention in America."

Dr. Unda Murillo received a great ovation for his valiant speech. Later he was applauded by thousands when he was invited to put the ball in play at a football game. When he descended to the field he received a tremendous ovation, which was, he said, as much for Guatemala as for himself.

When Dr. Unda Murillo and I talked over these matters he said that he took the ovation as the confirmation of approval of Guatemala's clearly defined anti-Communist policy.

IV

Jacobo Arbenz continued to thunder at us from Havana. On September 2 the Associated Press reported him as addressing the students of the National University and telling them that his mistake had been:

". . . not to execute the assassins employed by ex-dictator Jorgé Ubico. We did not execute those criminals and in 1954 they returned to kill our students, workers and peasants."

He solemnly pledged that the "next" government of Guatemala would execute all such criminals following the bright example of Fidel Castro who shot Cuban "war criminals."

A few days later, on September 7, 1960, the same international news agency reported that Arbenz, in a press conference, said:

". . . my guide in this revolution is Fidel Castro, and all

he has accomplished in Cuba since he achieved power, I will
do when I am again president of Guatemala."

The report describes Arbenz' face "glowed with menace"
when he added:

". . . all those cut-throats at the service of President Ydígoras Fuentes, who is the unconditional lackey of Yankee imperialism, will be sent to the wall."

On this occasion he again confirmed that he repented that
he lost control of Guatemala through his error in not arming
the militias and for having tolerated enemies whom he could
have summarily executed, just as Fidel Castro did, by sending
them to the wall, as a needed prologue to establishing a Socialist government. The reporter says that "he made it clear it was
his intention to recuperate the presidency of Guatemala."

Our air patrols succeeded in discouraging the sloop,
Theresa, from approaching the Guatemalan coast, but we
learned that a frigate, the *Liberty,* had sailed for Guatemala
from Cuba.

We heard more about the Yugoslavian guerrilla recruits and
even received a list of their names.

Commercial pilots who were fumigating cotton plantings
on the Pacific Coast again reported the mysterious submarine
that was plying just off our shores.

We found a powerful demolition bomb on a bridge near
Palo Gordo in the Pacific slopes, and it was removed without
achieving any damage.

Our intelligence kept us advised that Castro agents, spread
out over Central America, had instructions to provoke disorder and blood-mutinies. We learned that the guerrilla instructions had been almost completed and that legionnaires
from Poland, Czechoslovakia, Yugoslavia, among them, gradu-
ates of the terrorist school at Toulon, France, were already in
Cuba.

These men were chosen with great care, to assure success
along the designs of Soviet imperialism in Central America.
After the experience acquired in the lost battles of Latin
America (Orestes in Brazil and Arbenz in Guatemala) the

Communists turned to the theories that brought Mao Tse-tung to power in China. This consists of propaganda, agitation, use of students and international figures, etc., in order to embark on the campaign to conquer our hemisphere. The Soviets had skillfully converted Cuba into a springboard from which to leap into Central America.

A revolutionary congressman protested my many denunciations of invasions of Guatemala and ridiculed my warnings. "There is no invasion of the national territory of Guatemala," he said.

The great puzzle was made up of many small details: Word came from Montevideo that the family of Arbenz had given up its palatial residence and taken rooms in the Nagaro Hotel, evidently in preparation for a sudden departure from Uruguay.

Our aviators continued their patrols and on October 3 accosted the Cuban sloop *La Cubana,* which failed to heed their signals. The vessel was fired upon because we had information that it carried arms for the Guatemalan subversives. The vessel went aground on the Mexican island of Cozumel, off the coast of Yucatan. The sloop flew the Cuban flag, but we heard not one single word from Cuba regarding this incident. It was a guilty silence, indeed.

By the 3rd of October we had a pretty good idea that something was going to happen very soon. I attempted to forestall the movement and discourage the participants by publishing all that we knew, hinting that much more information was being kept back, for reasons of security. On that day I published the following bulletin:

SUBVERSIVE MOVEMENT FOR OCTOBER

Analysis as of September 28, 1960

DATE: The mobilization of the participants will begin on October 10. There will be landings on Honduran soil at the ports of Omoa and La Barra between October 10 and 15.

OBJECTIVES: Political:
1. Overthrow the present government.
2. Establishment of a Castro type regime.
3. Keep the United States from establishing bases on Guatemalan soil.

Military:
1. Military Zone of Puerto Barrios.
2. Military Zone of Coban.
3. Military Zone of Mazatenango.

TACTICS: Political agitation and disorders in the capital. Hit-and-run attacks. Guerrillas in the mountains.

TROOPS: North front: guerrillas in the mountains of Senahu, Purulha, Coban and Izabal (Las Quebradas). Central front: armed peasants in the Departments of Esquintla and Santa Rosa. South front: guerrillas in Nueva Concéption, Tiquisate, La Maquina.

COMMAND: North front, Colonel Carlos A. Paz Tejada; South front, Lieutenant Guillermo Lavagnino Higueros and Marco Antonio Villamar Contreras.

OTHER: Investigations have established that there is an illegal radio station operating in the Senahu region, it maintains contact with Cuba. The guerrillas of the north front will establish their headquarters in Senahu or Purulha. The military base at Puerto Barrios will be attacked. Lieutenant Lavagnino is now in Puerto Cortes waiting for the landings.

By letting the subversives know that we knew their leaders

and were in possession of their plans we discouraged the invasion.

Yet the aggressive plans were not completely abandoned.

Our intelligence discovered six innocent-looking boxes of canned grated coconut, packed in Cuba, on a beach on the Pacific Coast, during its careful combing of the district after the sighting of the mysterious submarine. The cartons were transferred to Guatemala City and their excessive weight aroused suspicion. When one of the cans was opened it was found to contain a complete hand grenade; manufactured in Czechoslovakia, ready for use with the detonator and explosive.

I suggested that the Minister of Foreign Relations make this known to the diplomatic corps and to both the local and foreign press, as it was conclusive proof of Cuban-Soviet designs on Guatemala.

All the accredited ambassadors, ministers and chargé d'affaires in Guatemala were invited to come to the office of the Minister of Foreign Relations on the 13th of October, and they accepted the invitation, including the United States Ambassador, John J. Muccio.

They were shown a sealed carton which was opened before their eyes to reveal twenty-four cans with the label "La Estrella," and the legend that they contained grated coconut in syrup manufactured by "Cuba Industrial y Commercial, S.A."

The group was invited to choose one can at random. It was opened before their eyes and found to contain a hand grenade carefully packed in sawdust, just as we had said. All the other cans were opened. Each one yielded a grenade.

9

THE NATIONAL LIBERATION MOVEMENT

I

MEANWHILE the Castro-Communist influence became stronger every day, especially in the capital. I was obliged to maintain myself constantly on the defensive. While my opponents did not increase their ranks, their aggressiveness—fired by the gold and propaganda from Cuba—each day became bolder.

The attack was so dangerous that I was obliged to take the offensive. I had talks with groups of Cuban exiles and with nations that were friendly towards them. We drew up a plan of action against those who had transformed Cuba into a detention camp and a base to corrupt America.

Representatives of the United States came to see me about training the Cuban anti-Castro forces and we came to a spoken agreement. My government granted permission for the training of Cuban contingents and for the massing of arms and planes on Guatemalan soil. The entire training program was in the hands of American officers assigned to the task, and the troops were entirely Cuban patriots.

While the matter of the failure of the invasion of Cochinos Bay has been amply discussed and there is little to add to that controversy as of this date, I would like to say, that in my opinion, the attitude of the United States press played a great part in dooming the operation. Hordes of reporters fell on Guatemala, in a veritable witch-hunt, and they seemed to have the single aim of exposing the attack. In this they were extraordinarily successful. If the United States press had maintained patriotic discretion, perhaps certain decisions taken by the White House in the most crucial moments of the attack on Cuba could have been different and today Cuba would be free and America would breathe easier.

II

In Guatemala the controversy regarding the anti-Cuban bases became a weapon in the hands of the Castro-Communists. During the last months of 1960 they used the existence of the bases to corrupt the Army. Officers were told that the preparations were not aimed against Cuba, but that I was building up a mercenary army to replace and substitute the national army. Such a fiction could only convince those who had never renounced their allegiance to communism or who were willing to justify low actions by sophism.

Many of my advisers criticized my decision to permit the Cuban forces to train with American arms and under American instructors on Guatemalan soil. They said it was a two-edged sword that threatened Guatemala as much as it did Cuba. In truth, all the Guatemalan revolutionary Reds opposed the move because they are always in agreement with Russia on two points of its foreign policy: absolute hatred of anything that smacks of the United States and blind obedience to Castro-Communist orders.

III

We knew and we were prepared for the offensive. At three o'clock Sunday morning, November 13, 1960, I was wakened by acting Chief of Staff, Colonel Francisco Ortiz. I had spent the night in the second city of Guatemala, Quezaltenango, where I had officiated certain ceremonies and visited new industries.

I was informed that the "Justo Rufino Barracks" in Guatemala City had rebelled. This was the inevitable military movement to complement the long months of political agitation. It was fired by the presence of the anti-Castro contingents in Guatemala.

The leaders of the Army faction were four colonels, a major, two captains and two lieutenants. It was not surprising that of the ring leaders, three were students in the Law Faculty of the University of San Carlos, the veritable incubating area for communism in Guatemala.

One of the leaders, Lieutenant Colonel Rafael Sesan Pereira, had just been relieved of his duties as supply officer of the "Justo Rufino Barracks" and he was to surrender his command on the very night the uprising took place. Proof had been presented to me that he was receiving money from Cuba, via Mexico. Proof was not sufficient to submit him to trial, but it was sufficient to remove him from a post of confidence. His subsequent actions confirmed my suspicions.

Two of the younger officers, Captain Arturo Chur del Cid and Lieutenant Marco Antonio Yon Sosa, were under arrest in the same barracks for minor disciplinary faults. They had sought arrest in order to be in the barracks at the appointed time, as their regular stations were elsewhere.

Lieutenant Colonel Sesan Pereira gave them the freedom of the barracks and they won a number of non-commissioned officers and enlisted men to their cause with promises of money and other rewards. The conspirators maintained contact with the political groups through Sesan Pereira.

His unexpected dismissal led Sesan Pereira to precipitate events. He made personal contact with Colonel Carlos Paz Tejada and Marco Antonio Villamar Contreras, the true military and civilian leaders of the movement. He told them that the action would take place on the night of November 12 and demanded the promised political and popular support. Both Tejada and Contreras protested that the movement would be premature because the political preparation and popular support was not ready. Sesan Pereira was adamant—perhaps fearful that his days of liberty were limited, seeing his dismissal as the handwriting on the wall—he replied that it was impossible to postpone the action because the order had been given.

IV

Sesan Pereira was at his post in the barracks on the night of November 12, 1960. He surreptitiously conversed with his fellow plotters and the plan was set in motion.

At about two o'clock in the morning of the 13th two men in civilian dress approached the entrance to the barracks. The guards were amazed when the two men gave the correct countersign when challenged. The Officer of the Guard, Captain Juarez Mayen, was informed by telephone. From their description the men were identified as army officers, Lieutenant Colonel Vicente Loarca Argueta and Second Lieutenant Zelada Rodriguez. Captain Juarez Mayen ordered the guards to arrest them and to take them to the Command Post. He then went personally to the quarters of the Third Chief, Colonel Arreaga Hernandez to make his report.

When Captain Juarez Mayen left his post, Captain Arturo Chur del Cid, who had been under arrest, presented himself at the Command Post, accompanied by two men, all armed with machine guns, and threatened the sergeant of the guard and the others with their weapons. They were told to obey instructions or die.

At that moment Captain Juarez Mayen came running back to the command post calling out: "What's going on here!"

Sergeant Hector Werner Fernandez Cruz, one of the men with del Cid, loosed a clip at the Captain, who staggered into the Command Post, bleeding copiously. He died instantly.

Fernandez Cruz then ran towards the door of the bedroom of the Executive Officer, Colonel José Ortiz Cordova, expecting him to come out. This is exactly what happened. Colonel Ortiz appeared at the door with a question on his lips. Sergeant Fernandez Cruz cynically replied, "All is well," and shot him dead.

V

Colonel Juan B. Martinez was officer of the day at the old presidential palace, now used for certain offices of the Presidency and for the presidential army staff. An FM radio operator named Franco, on duty, heard the shots in the "Justo Rufino Barrios Barracks" and immediately reported them to his chief. When Colonel Martinez was unable to contact the barracks by telephone (the lines had been cut), he advised the Minister of Defense, the National Police and the acting commander of the presidential guard of honor, Colonel Gildardo Monzon.

The providential alertness of radio operator Franco informed us of the events minutes after they transpired. One hour later I was aroused from my sleep.

After I had secured the situation in Quezaltenango, making certain that no focus of insurrection was present there, I flew back to the capital. The report I received was perplexing. The rebels had packed troops, weapons and supplies onto every available vehicle, commandeered the armored cars, and abandoned the capital. The police post at the point where the highway to the North Atlantic Coast and Puerto Barrios entered the city reported that a convoy had passed. Later word came that a toll station along the highway had been assaulted and the funds stolen.

Between the convoy and the Caribbean port was the second military zone of Guatemala at the railway junction of Zacapa. I assumed personal command of the armed forces and established my headquarters at La Aurora Air Force Base. My first orders were that armed Mustangs patrol the North Atlantic highway and locate the convoy. It was sighted around eight o'clock approaching the "Carrera" barracks at Zacapa.

Word had reached me that at 6:30 on that morning two light planes had flown over Zacapa and dropped thousands of handbills inciting the people to support a revolutionary movement. The commander of the military base, Colonel Gonzalez Monroy, had organized resistance and disposed troops at different points. Unfortunately, some of these were party to the plot and did not occupy the appointed stations. The convoy was able to enter the barracks by announcing that they were "reinforcements" sent from the capital. In fact, the troops that had been impressed were informed that their mission was to defend the government.

The personnel of the barracks was overpowered, without combat, and the officers were placed under arrest. The chief of police of Zacapa, who had been unable to contact the barracks by telephone, personally went to the barracks, and was also taken prisoner.

By eleven o'clock in the morning I loosed the first fire on the rebels. Armed planes strafed the barracks with machine gun fire and rockets. When the first B-26 bombers returned to refuel and replenish their ammunition they reported that a column of men had been sighted marching towards the neighboring city of Chiquimula and were disbanded by an aerial attack.

I had no communication with Zacapa, Puerto Barrios, nor any of the important bases in the north of the country. A little after lunch, on the 13th, I received a visit from the President of the National Congress. He said that a congressman had asked him if he had collected his salary for October; saying that he "had better get it because it would be the last" he would draw as President of Congress.

Infantry troops were sent to recuperate Zacapa. These were placed under the orders of Colonel Peralta Azurdia, then Minister of Agriculture, later to become Minister of Defense.

Around 3,000 men were prepared for the attack on Zacapa, not that we believed that such a large number was needed to subdue the rebels, but because we saw the possibility of reinforcements reaching the rebels from across the Honduran border and by sea through Puerto Barrios from Cuba.

The President of neighboring Honduras disarmed and detained a group of over 150 guerrillas that attempted to cross the border into Guatemala in the Chiquimula area, undoubtedly intending to join the column dispatched from Zacapa that was disrupted.

We continued our air attack on Zacapa for several hours. The rebels took up positions in the hills. Anti-aircraft fire revealed their presence.

Planes had patrolled over Puerto Barrios and they had been fired on. This meant that the Air Base at Puerto Barrios was also in the hands of the rebels.

Our attack on Zacapa continued at dawn on the 14th. By four o'clock in the afternoon the anti-aircraft fire and fire from the Army Base was silenced. The first loyal men to enter the barracks was a squad of machine gunners under the command of Major José Dolores Argueta. The rebels fled towards the Honduran border taking with them a good amount of arms.

VI

Puerto Barrios had been captured by the rebels. Army officers took advantage of their rank to enter the military installations and once inside had subjected their fellow officers to threats and imprisonment.

Mario René Chavez Garcia, a politician, who had traveled to Cuba and returned with Castro insignias, which he gave to "persons of complete confidence" saying they would be useful "later on," showed up at Puerto Barrios. This port, of course, has a large laboring population; for the most part dock workers. These men had been wooed by the previous revolutionary governments and it was believed that they would be receptive to Communist ideas. A manifesto was distributed by Garcia reminding them that they had been exploited for decades.

"We are not alone," it said. "The entire nation is with us: intellectuals, workers, students; in other words, all the vital forces of the nation; and *we have the support and the cooperation of a free country, which is truly sovereign, that shoulder to shoulder with Guatemalan workers . . . will help us,* the true representatives of the Army, to expulse from our soil those despoilers who take everything and leave only hunger and misery in their wake."

All Sunday afternoon the base was strafed. We concentrated on the landing strip aiming to make the field inoperative and to preclude the possibility of assistance arriving by air. Subjected to the fierce attack, and with no sign of the promised assistance, the rebels contacted me by radio telephone through the Tropical Radio installations that they had captured. They asked for a parley and I sent Pilot Major Marco Antonio Batres and two other officers in my Aero Commander plane. Instead of talking terms the rebels captured the emissaries.

Major Batres returned alone. He said that the rebel leader had ordered him to fly him to Zacapa, from where no word had been received. Batres agreed, under pressure, but with the excuse of tuning up the motors, he had taken off to report. The two other men were hostages and we ceased attack on the Puerto Barrios base.

On the afternoon of the 14th our radio operator in Poptun, a little post in the Peten rain forests, received the following message repeatedly:

TO THE REVOLUTIONARIES OF PUERTO BARRIOS
FROM CUBA.

As the Puerto Barrios base has been destroyed the promised assistance has not arrived, but it will arrive soon.—375.

A force was sent overland to Puerto Barrios, the air attacks had not been continued in order to protect the lives of the two hostages. I received reports that two planes had flown over the little hamlet of Livingston, across the sound from Puerto Barrios. We later found several bundles of arms that had been parachuted from these planes.

VII

The rebel leader in Puerto Barrios, Colonel Llerena Muller, became uneasy in view of Zacapa's silence. Obviously it had not been his plan to capture the port of Puerto Barrios and to set up an independent republic there. He was caught between the devil and the deep blue sea. I imagine he kept his eyes hopefully on the waters of the Bay of Amatique, on which Puerto Barrios lies; but, our well-armed frigate had cast off when warned by radio and it stood by to discourage any invasion attempt.

The possibility of assistance from Cuba had become remote indeed. I had called on President Eisenhower to help us protect our coasts and he had dispatched the aircraft carrier "Shanghri-La" to maintain a strategic patrol of the Caribbean.

When Llerena Muller was unable to make contact with Zacapa, he made up his mind to go there himself—his judgement and nerves were failing. He made up a convoy of trucks and accompanied by ten officers and a contingent of men, he set off up the North Atlantic road. When they arrived at an intersection called Entrerios they saw planes overhead, flying towards Barrios. The convoy stopped and one of the officers stated that "all was lost." According to reports received later it seems that it was suggested that some of the officers use the telephone to call for reinforcements. It did not occur to Llerena Muller to inquire where the reinforcements would come from. The officers were granted permission to undertake the mission. Llerena Muller watched their dust and waited patiently for their return. The officers did not come back. Eighty men deserted with them.

The plague of desertions extended itself when Llerena Muller returned to Puerto Barrios with his depleted convoy. This was the beginning of the end of the Revolutionary Command of the Atlantic.

That night the rebels held another mass meeting. The political leader, Chavez Garcia, had been able to recruit over 300 civilians, but what these civilians witnessed served to cool their ardor.

One of the captured pilots was Colonel Alfonso Giron Beteta. He was obliged to address the meeting. His address was neither appealing nor intelligible. All the while he spoke, a .45 was pushed into his ribs.

While the meeting was being held, taking advantage of the absence of the ring leaders and the little sympathy of the impressed troops for the cause, the other pilots were able to escape. One of them was able to reach the United Fruit Company offices at Bananera and there he informed me over the telephone that all the hostages were free.

I immediately ordered that the Puerto Barrios base be subjected to a heavy air attack. Overland the infantry was fast approaching its objective. It engaged enemy troops at a town called Gualan. The battle was a rout for the rebels.

Before one single loyal soldier arrived at the port or one of our planes landed at the base, the Supreme Commander of the Revolutionary Commandos of the Atlantic appropriated a blue station wagon, and accompanied by a few officers, made for the Honduran border. His flight was emulated by all the other leaders and Puerto Barrios was no longer the General Headquarters of the National Liberation Movement, nor was there any movement.

It so happened that a young pilot, Captain Guillermo Mendoza, had recently left the Military to work for an American oil company. He was in Puerto Barrios and when he witnessed the flight of the leaders, and saw machine guns, rifles, grenades and all manner of weapons in the hands of civilians; subject to no leader; many of them ruffians, he appointed himself my representative and took command of the troops.

A telephone call informed me of these events; a Mustang was sent to investigate and returned to say that an immense crowd was gathered at the airport and that white sheets had been placed on the ground alongside the landing strip.

I went to Puerto Barrios with four transports of troops. We organized a mop-up operation, requisitioning a number of trucks. In a matter of hours we had cleaned the area of rebels.

VIII

The "national liberation movement" was over. It had cost Guatemala much—in lives, property, supplies, money and illusions. The local and international press were incredulous as to the hand of international communism in the affair.

To those who understand that the immediate objective of the Communist strategy is to provoke political or revolutionary action by sympathetic non-Communists, for the purpose of establishing an environment within which the Communist Party is free to organize and expand, the chain of events are proof enough in themselves.

When such a movement triumphs, a new Soviet base is established. When it fails, as it did in Guatemala, then it is the hungry, down-trodden, neglected, abused population clamoring for social justice; or the idealistic youth of the Army seeking progress.

However, the entire picture, starting with the urgent objective of destroying the anti-Cuban bases in Guatemala; the seemingly pointless overpowering of a barracks in the capital to flee with the arms to the coast; the knowledge that Colonel Rafael Sesan Pereira was receiving money from Cuba that caused his dismissal; the intervention of the known Communist Mario René Chavez Garcia; the admission in the revolutionary manifesto that "a free country, which is truly sovereign" gave the movement support and cooperation; the intercepted message from Cuba; and the fact that the movement was the culmination of months of political agitation are all powerful indications that the movement was not Guatemalan in its essence.

True enough, dissatisfied groups are entitled to brief spasms of rebellion. Taken out of context, the uprising of November 13, 1960, is just this. But, placed in its proper relation to events within Guatemala and the world, it acquires a broader meaning.

10

GUATEMALA AT
PUNTA DEL ESTE

I

The Seventh Consultative Meeting of Foreign Ministers took place at Punta del Este between January 22 and 31, 1962. It was called for by Colombia under the Inter-American Treaty of Reciprocal Assistance (known as the Rio Treaty) to consider threats against the peace and political independence of the American states that may arise from the intervention of extracontinental powers to disrupt American solidarity.

The possibility of a strong condemnation of Cuba at this meeting was none too likely. We knew from the outset that a unanimous vote could not be achieved on a strong measure against Cuba. A watered-down, or "soft measure," could be achieved by unanimity—with the certain exception of Cuba voting against or abstaining. But as President of Guatemala I definitely did not want this. It was my firm conviction that weakness in action would destroy the Organization. It was already showing signs of deterioration. I was determined that a strong resolution against Cuba emanate from the meeting.

Foreign Minister Unda Murillo went personally; and I wrote letters, sent emissaries, talked on the telephone, and thus we were able to have the five countries of Central America and Panama agree to attend the Punta del Este meeting as a single bloc. United by our common preoccupation over the intervention of Castro-communism within our borders, we were determined to present a closely-knit front, that could influence the larger but more timid countries which were unwilling to recommend drastic measures against Castro because of the immense fifth columns maintained by the Communists in their countries.

Because Guatemala had taken the initiative, Dr. Unda Murillo was chosen as spokesman for the bloc. While we were the most united group of nations, at the same time we were the smallest territorially. However, when Dr. Unda Murillo addressed the assembly all knew that he was not speaking for Guatemala alone, but also for El Salvador, Honduras, Nicaragua, Costa Rica and Panama.

Brazil and Mexico had already declared that they would not adhere to any resolution condemning Cuba, and Ecuador and Bolivia were of the same mind. Two-thirds majority was necessary for the "hard" measure we desired, or a total of fourteen votes against seven.

Thirteen American nations had broken relations with Cuba prior to the meeting. These were: United States, Guatemala, El Salvador, Dominican Republic, Colombia, Venezuela, Nicaragua, Costa Rica, Honduras, Panama, Peru, Paraguay and Haiti. Despite optimism expressed in the United States press prior to the meeting, the prospects were none too bright.

Against a harsh measure were seven nations: Brazil, Mexico, Argentina, Ecuador, Bolivia, Chile, and Cuba, and an eighth nation, surprisingly enough, proclaimed its neutrality although it had broken off relations with Cuba: Haiti.

It was thus that I dispatched the Guatemalan delegation to Punta del Este, under the leadership of Dr. Unda Murillo, with instructions to move heaven and earth to obtain effective and practical measures against the de facto government of Fidel Castro. On December 1, 1961, Fidel Castro had said:

. . . We are in the phase of building a socialist society. And socialism, which is the socialism that we are to apply, utopian socialism? It is merely a matter of applying scientific socialism. That is why I said at the beginning, with complete frankness, that we believed in Marxism, that we believed it was the most valid theory, the most scientific, the only true theory; the only true revolutionary; yes, I say it here with complete satisfaction, and with complete confidence.

I am a Marxist-Leninist and I will be a Marxist-Leninist until the last day of my life.

This was the banner under which President Osvaldo Dorticos of Cuba took his seat at the Eighth Consultative Meeting of Foreign Ministers of American States.

II

The proceedings of an international meeting of this kind are intricate and involved; the reports cover hundreds of pages; hundreds of thousands of words are spoken and recorded. Newsmen report the highlights, or what they believe to be the highlights, to their principals. However, only painstaking analysis of the actual proceedings can bring to light the most important forces and currents at work.

The meetings follow a strict protocol; each delegation is allowed a principal address and may speak again under certain circumstances. The policies of each delegation are expressed in their public utterances, but the true currents of such an assembly are seen in the resolutions that are presented and in the work that goes on behind closed doors.

The opening address, aside from the formal utterances of protocol, was given by the Minister of Foreign Relations of Colombia, Dr. José Joaquin Caicedo, on January 24. Although the meeting had been convoked at the request of Colombia, the Minister said: "We have no offenses to ventilate before the concert of our brothers of America." He mentioned the suspension of relations with Cuba but said: "We have no specific controversy with this State." Colombia did not support Cuba but said that the problem before the conference was: ". . . to ascertain if the principle of non-intervention was threatened, by the existence of a national regime whose concept of law, whose political philosophy, whose subordination to a different system, are incompatible with the Organization that the American States have created."

He did, however, condemn the Cuban government in the following words: "We do not doubt that a Cuban Communist regime must necessarily undertake, as other Soviet powers would, to destroy the Inter-American system and to procure, by any means, but preferably by force, the extension of the Communist revolution in our hemisphere." The Colombian Minister then proposed certain measures calling for reaffirmation of the principles of inter-American solidarity and for a detailed study of the question of incompatibility. This of course was a good opening attack.

It was then the moment for my Foreign Minister to address the assembly. He did so in a straightforward, undisguised assault on Cuba. Those present knew his voice interpreted the sentiments of all the Central American nations, and Panama:

"Without euphemisms or dissembling, we speak clearly of Cuba, of the marvellous Caribbean Isle that unhappily today is shackled, enslaved, tyrannized, not by one of those native dictatorships, that one good day become over-ripe, and rot, and fall from inertia; but by an iron-clad international imposition. Of course, when I speak of this tragedy it will be said that we are 'agents of Yankee imperialism on the payroll of the State Department,' or 'pawns of the Colonial Office,' as this Organization is often termed by the pawns of Sino-Soviet imperialism in America; thus offending the dignity of each and all of its members by such epithets. The regime that usurps power in Cuba, intervened and interventionist, has openly and shamelessly proclaimed itself Communist, and is submissive to the dictates of the Sino-Soviets in the aim to impose similar systems on the other countries of America, thus serving as the vanguard for the gloomy designs of that imperialism."

He quoted Mr. Guevara as saying, on May 8, 1961:

" 'The Cuban revolution has set an example for the peoples of America. The masses now know how it is done . . . There are many who distrust their power. They fear imperialism. Although they knew, as we all know, that the first step was to destroy all the servants of the empire, but they did not know how to do it. Later, they found out that the masses are so created that they will inevitably achieve power, if not peacefully, through violence. They learned that in America there is a way, certainly not the only way, but a way that has shown its efficiency, and that is guerrilla warfare. They had then a path open to them.' "

Dr. Unda Murillo continued:

"The Cuban situation represents an authentic threat to the collective security of America . . . *non-intervention, auto-determination and the juridic equality of states?* The hour has struck for America to speak openly. We are horrified when intervention is mentioned. I declare categorically in the name of the people of Guatemala that the principle of non-intervention of one state in the affairs of another should be defended at all costs if we do not want to return to international violence, to anarchy, abuse and chaos. But, Honorable Chancellors, let us not fool ourselves, let us not put things out of joint, let us not exaggerate our philosophies, nor distort them. Powerful international forces, powerful extra-continental governments *have* intervened in Cuba, and continue to intervene in Cuba, with the shameless complicity of its government, that through deceit and through force illegally holds the destiny of the Cuban people in its grasp.

"Meanwhile, we, seated in our offices, with our arms

crossed, continue to twist our own juridic arguments, to bring them to maximum perfection; while the others: the daring, the inhuman, the soulless, who have no God, nor law, nor country; come into our yards, into our homes, dealing resounding kicks at our sacred principles of non-intervention and auto-determination.

"There are those who pretend that the convocation of this consultative meeting is 'an open intromission into the principle of non-intervention.' Let us analyze that intervention dispassionately, without slurs or disquisitions of a politico-philosophical nature; or better said: Who are intervening? Can our firm decision to defend ourselves against those who attempt to destroy our democratic institutions be called intervention? Against those who conspire to overthrow legitimate governments and to deliver us into the hands of the vandalic hordes of Red imperialism?

"This eighth meeting . . . should not permit the banner of non-intervention to be lifted hypocritically to cover up a shameless and ominous intervention, nor to permit unfounded scruples to paralyze the Organization and to keep it from taking opportune and efficient measures before the Cuban situation.

"It is painful to observe the suicidal attitude of the Organization. While on the one hand the principle of non-intervention is invoked to keep the Organization from taking measures against Cuba, in defense of the Organization and to guarantee its continued existence, on the other hand it is tolerated that Russia and China have absolute control over Cuba and permission is intended to those who have assaulted power in that country to export their Marxist-Leninist revolution to other American nations; and what is more serious, to support filibuster invasions, terrorist acts, and sedition, as has occurred in the Dominican Republic, Panama, Haiti, Nicaragua, and Guatemala."

These and many other truths were presented for the consideration of the delegates and in the name of the Government of Guatemala, he called for:

1) The energetic condemnation of the regime that governs Cuba on the grounds that it was subject to international communism, and for its constant intervention in the internal affairs of the other American nations, which was incompatible with the principles and aims of the inter-American system and a serious threat and grave danger to the peace and security of the continent.

2) To deny Cuba representation in the different bodies of the Organization.

3) The breaking off of relations of all the member states with Cuba.

4) The breaking off of economic relations of all the member states with Cuba.

5) And the immediate suspension of traffic in arms and implements of warfare between the American republics and Cuba.

He ended our condemnation of Cuba with the following words:

"We must now act and take firm decisions. We are obliged to do this by the universal and deafening clamor of millions of enslaved peoples . . . our responsibility before the destiny of the world is serious. The fate of the Organization of American States is now in our hands. On taking our decision we must act with decision, courage, and faith. We must do it to rescue the sublime American ideals and with them the ideals of the world, and liberty, that has cost so dearly and so much blood. We must also do it for our children, for whom we foresee a future of peace, security and dignity. The founders of America demand it of us in this historic moment. Faith and hope in our common destiny. In liberty that gives us dignity and elevates us. In one word: *Faith,* in our home-lands and in God!"

It would seem that after such an impassioned and frank intervention, every democratic voice would be raised to support our measures. But immediately after, the Foreign Minister of Mexico, Manuel Tello, spoke as follows:

"Fortunately, for myself and my fellow delegates, we come to Punta del Este in a moment when not the slightest shadow clouds the sincere and frank ties that unite Mexico with the nations of this hemisphere."

He openly said that in his opinion "the convocation lacked juridic basis . . ." and through his intervention it was evident that Mexico was not going to change her announced position.

The Colombian Delegation proposed a measure that did not mention Cuba, although it clearly outlined the threat that existed to the independence of the hemisphere.

The Bolivian delegate spoke of the Bolivian "revolution" and maintained the position of neutrality of his country.

The Brazilian delegate came out against sanctions of any kind, military or political, and proposed a very weak measure.

On the following day, the 25th, other delegations spoke; some nations aligning themselves with Guatemala, and others maintaining their stand against us. The Haitian delegate stated the position of his country in a few words:

"The people of Haiti, who have maintained themselves neutral during the Caribbean imbroglio, continue to cleave to its neutrality, and will have the audacity to not renounce this vocation, and to deny support to one or the other."

Ecuador stated its position thus:

"Nevertheless, to obtain favorable resolutions of the democratic thesis of America, what we should seek is a system that permits solution of the problem of incompatibility, heretofore expressed, it being impossible to apply sanctions of any kind at this moment because the juridic statute is insufficient; neither men nor peoples are sanctioned for what they think of doing, nor for their intentions; but for acts that they have committed. What can be done is to take preventive measures

... and these cannot be determined by [the Rio Treaty]."

Argentina chose to defend the principle of non-intervention in reverse:

"We are united here to take up an international question that is reflected with different projections and disparate import in the American society. With this point of view and with this sense of responsibility we must seek harmonious solutions . . . Argentina does not desire nor does it intend to intervene in the internal affairs of Cuba."

Paraguay condemned "international communism for having used the most diverse methods of aggressive interventionism to subjugate Paraguay." Raúl Sapena Pastor, the Foreign Minister of Paraguay, outlined numerous incidents of intervention, many similar to those that are described as occurring in Guatemala.

III

Behind the scenes momentous events were taking place, of which I was fully informed. Our delegation spoke for the five countries of Central America, Panama, Peru, Paraguay, and the Dominican Republic. In the private meetings, several of the Ministers who advocated the "soft line" presented different formulas, in which the government of Fidel Castro came out with advantages and benefits it did not even have when the conference was opened. These were rejected by the Guatemalan and Colombian Delegates.

The United States delegation was among those that were supporting the "soft" group. Foreign Minister Unda Murillo informed me of the situation and I immediately cabled him:

I BELIEVE THAT PAN AMERICANISM SHOULD PREVAIL AND THAT ITS INSTITUTIONS SHOULD BE UNANIMOUSLY DEFENDED BY ALL NATIONS, BOTH LARGE AND SMALL STOP BUSINESS MEN HAVING SHADY INTERESTS AND

WHO LACK SCRUPLES PREFER TO DO BUSINESS IN TIMES
WHEN A 400% PROFIT CAN BE ACHIEVED INSTEAD OF
DEFENDING CHRISTIAN AND DEMOCRATIC PRINCIPLES
STOP DEFEND THEM EVEN IF YOU REMAIN ALONE STOP.

With this, Foreign Minister Unda Murillo had a private talk with Dean Rusk, the United States Secretary of State who headed the United States delegation.

He informed Dean Rusk that Guatemala preferred that the meeting be suspended completely, and threatened to withdraw the Guatemalan delegation rather than be obliged to accept a proposal and assume a position that was completely opposite to our convictions.

The United States wanted a unanimous measure, even if it was a weak one; we wanted a strong measure, even if it was not unanimous. This was our struggle.

Dean Rusk was a magnificent negotiator, he was patient with all of us and finally he accepted the view of the nations that supported the strong measure.

Of extreme importance, as I was later informed by Foreign Minister Unda Murillo, was the determined attitude of certain other delegations: those of El Salvador, Honduras, Nicaragua, Costa Rica, Panama, Peru, Paraguay, and the Dominican Republic. Our position was so secure that during his historic talks with Dean Rusk, the United States delegate, Dr. Unda Murillo said that if Guatemala were to withdraw from the conference, she would not withdraw alone, but that other countries would follow our example.

In my opinion the conciliatory attitude of the United States at this time was due to Mr. Rusk's advisors, who held that a soft resolution, supported by all twenty nations, was preferable to a strong resolution with only fourteen votes.

We believe that Mr. Rusk's change of heart was due in large part to the determined attitude of our delegation and to the possibility that nations would abandon the conference if a strong resolution was not approved.

The President of Cuba, Osvaldo Dorticos, spoke disparagingly of Foreign Minister Unda Murillo, saying:

"I am not going to imitate, for example, the Guatemalan representative, nor will arrogance characterize my address."

He attacked the representative democratic system and all its institutions. He said that far from being an aggressor nation, Cuba was the victim of aggression, and he cited my speech of December 31, 1961, in which I had acknowledged Guatemala's part in the attack on Cuba, at the Bay of Pigs.

However, we now had thirteen delegations committed to a strong sanction against Cuba. Only one vote was still missing for the necessary two-thirds majority. Everything humanly possible had been done to sway Haiti, the avowedly "neutral" nation to our side.

Far from the scene of events, in Guatemala, I dictated a cablegram to our Ambassador in Port au Prince, ordering that it be coded, but unfortunately my instructions were misunderstood, and it was sent in plain language, the first word of the text being "Code." It read more or less as follows:

CODE: It being proven that the illustrious government of Haiti has abandoned its brothers of the Caribbean at Punta del Este I have decided to definitely close our Embassy in that country, and I am hereby cautioning you that several other Central American countries will shortly follow our example. Prepare yourself to return to Guatemala and seek a friendly nation to take charge of our affairs in Haiti.

(signed) *President Ydígoras*

We did not have to wait long for a reply. The Haitian Chancellery read the message, and our friend, his Excellency, President Duvalier, reacted at once and ordered his Delegation to change its tactics. Thus it was that the fourteenth and deciding vote was assured in favor of the strong measure.

It is common knowledge that the exclusion of the present government of Cuba from participation in the inter-American system was approved by fourteen affirmative votes, one negative vote, and six abstentions.

As a matter of record, the six abstentions were those of Brazil, Mexico, Argentina, Ecuador, Bolivia and Chile, and the negative vote, of course, was that of Cuba.

However, the large nations never fulfilled what was resolved on that memorable occasion, and to the contrary, took advantage of the embargo imposed by the United States on Cuba to carry on illicit commerce and to ship to Cuba basic products needed for its maintenance.

But at any rate it was proven that the Guatemalans valiantly led the nations of the West on that occasion.

I was personally at the airport when the Guatemalan delegation returned and it was my pleasure to be the first to embrace Dr. Unda Murillo and to congratulate him on his valiant work. I told him that he had precisely interpreted my feelings in our war against communism.

He was modest and shared the honor with the other members of the Guatemalan delegation, whom I want to mention here:

Ambassador Luis Coronado Lira, Ambassador Carlos Urrutia Aparicio, Congressman José Garcia Bauer, Messrs. Alberto Arreaga, Isidoro Zarco and Justo Quijano.

When we were alone, Foreign Minister Unda Murillo told me that President Dorticos and his delegation had made declarations in Montevideo to newsmen, and over the radio and television systems, that very soon Guatemala, and the other countries that had voted against Castro, would feel the consequences of their attitude. "We are going to have some headaches here in Guatemala," he told me, "and we must be prepared."

Thus it was that in the close of the first months of 1962 these dramatic events took place at the historic meeting at Punta del Este.

11

DORTICOS KEEPS
HIS WORD

I

At eight p.m. on February 13, 1962, the powerful Red transmitters of Radio Havana carried the strident voice of Jacobo Arbenz over the Caribbean airwaves:

"A week ago today a handful of young patriots embarked on the glorious path of guerrilla warfare. The 'Alejandro de Leon' movement will end the rotted regime of the criminal traitors, accomplices of the corrupt and tyrannical Miguel Ydígoras Fuentes."

President Dorticos of Cuba had kept his word; the effects of our stand at Punta del Este were not long in being felt.

II

Izabal is one of the most isolated departments of Guatemala. It borders on the undeveloped Peten rain forests, the legendary home of the ancient Maya, and the Caribbean washes its southernmost shores. Lake Izabal, the largest in Guatemala, gives this department direct access to the Gulf of Amatique and the Caribbean, by way of the navigable, historic river Rio

Dulce, where pirates once took refuge and even today adventurers grapple for treasure.

Mariscos, a small Indian village on the banks of Lake Izabal, had been the base for a squad of riflemen. But at this time it was merely a post with a communications officer and six men. At five minutes to two on February 6th, the lone officer was preparing to bathe when he was overpowered by several armed men who had sneaked by the drowsy sentinel, nodding in the heat of the afternoon. They disarmed him, surrounded the post, and held the six loyal men at gunpoint.

Once the post was secured, the rebel officer fired a shot into the air and three trucks, filled with the balance of the rebel troops, rolled into the town.

The action lasted hardly ten minutes. The rebels destroyed the communications equipment, captured all the arms and ammunition, stole the clothes and personal effects of the officer and his men. They then withdrew along the route from which they had approached. They took no prisoners.

This bloodless action was the first assault.

The rebels then attacked Bananera, the division headquarters of the United Fruit Company on the Atlantic Coast of Guatemala. Sixty years earlier, this American company had been established to plant bananas for consumption in the United States. Over the years it grew rich and powerful and came to be the prime symbol of "Yankee imperialism" in the Caribbean Area. It was the same company that had been influential and generous in the formation and the financing of Castillo Armas' army of liberation, and with whom I had refused to cooperate.

Twelve officers preceded the rebel detachment in a truck and approached to within fifty meters of the Bananera military post. One of them advanced, unarmed, to the door of the post and talked for a few moments with the commandant, Second Lieutenant Zenon Reyna Gonzalez. Either by prior arrangement, or through some quick salesmanship, the Commandant agreed to surrender the post.

The balance of the rebel troops were then ordered to advance and the unsuspecting garrison allowed them to approach, under the impression that they were a relief detachment. But they were soon undeceived. One of the rebel officers then ordered the detachment to form ranks, backing up his order with a submachine gun. The sergeant of the guard was sufficiently alert to duck away and run to the Commandant crying out that the post was being "captured." The Commandant ordered him to keep cool, that there was nothing to worry about, that "they were his friends."

The leader of the rebels was an officer who had taken part in the uprising of November 16, 1960, and who had escaped over the border to Honduras: Marco Antonio Yon Sosa.

The surprised troops were disarmed and marched to several different trucks. Half of the men were ordered to board a truck that headed for Puerto Barrios, the other to board a truck that headed for Zacapa. Once the troops were in the trucks they were given back their arms and ammunition but warned that anyone who failed to obey orders, or deserted, would be summarily executed.

Bananera corresponds exactly to the novelistic image of the collection of sickly yellow bungalows on stilts, rising over enormous smooth lawns, in the shadow of palm trees, silhouetted against an azure, cloudless sky of a tropical paradise. It is the capital of the United Fruit Company's now ailing banana empire in Guatemala, and the entire settlement is on company land. Aside from the single bungalows for the first-class employees, there are several large buildings housing the administrative offices; and somewhere, across the tracks, the "yards" for the laborers and natives.

Lieutenant Marco Antonio Yon Sosa, Second Lieutenant Julio Bolanos San Juan, and two rebel soldiers marched along the neat cement walk to the building that housed the accounting department, and behind a menacing machine gun obliged the cashier to open the company safe. They stole $18,000.

Yon Sosa then picked up the telephone and managed to make contact with the military base at Zacapa. He told an officer that the military base should surrender by nine P.M. or it would be attacked. He then mounted a light truck, with his $18,000 victory in his hands, and started up the Atlantic Highway towards Guatemala City, with the intention of hiding in the capital.

The column that was supposed to attack Zacapa kept to the paved highway for a number of kilometers, then turned off onto a dirt road, at a place near Los Amates. The troops were ordered from the trucks and continued on foot to a chain of hills called the Sierra de las Minas, where they were told to prepare for combat. The group was reinforced with a number of civilians and was under the command of Second Lieutenant Ronald Pazos Rosal. The rebel officers held their positions until it was obvious that no reinforcements were coming. They did not enter into combat and made no attempt to carry out Yon Sosa's orders to attack the military base at Zacapa.

The troops that headed north, towards Puerto Barrios, were under the command of Second Lieutenant Zenon Reyna Gonzalez. These came to a point three kilometers from the port where the branch road to Puerto Matias de Galvez begins. A patrol from the Puerto Barrios military base was stationed at these crossroads and it stopped the first truck in which the rebels were traveling. One of the enlisted men approached the truck, fearlessly, and ordered the rebel officer, Reyna Gonzalez, to get out and report to the officer in charge of the squad before proceeding. The rebel attempted to deceive the soldier by alleging urgency, or some excuse not to stop, but did not succeed. The soldier who had advanced with his rifle in "ready" position, disarmed the rebel officer and conducted him towards the loyal troops. But at the very moment that Reyna Gonzalez was being interrogated by the loyal commander, the other rebel officer, Julio Bolanos San Juan, who had rolled up to the scene in another vehicle, ran towards the contingent of loyal troops, loosing a hail of fire from a submachine gun. The ensuing free-for-all lasted approximately fifteen minutes and the rebel Reyna Gonzalez was killed, as well as the commander of the loyal troops, Second Lieutenant Jorge Mario Ruano Galvez. The rebel officer, Julio Bolanos San Juan was wounded, as well as one rebel soldier and four loyal. The remaining rebels were placed under arrest.

Meanwhile, Yon Sosa had continued towards the capital, but his light truck broke down and he commandeered a public bus, leaving the passengers on foot. The general staff had been informed of events in the Izabal zone, and a squad of riflemen had been dispatched north in vehicles under the command of Major German Chupina Barahona. Not far from the point where the North Atlantic Highway and the branch road to Zacapa meet, the advance guard of loyal troops, under the command of Second Lieutenant Juan Bolanos Chavez, made contact with the rebels.

These were ordered to halt, and Bolanos Chavez walked towards the front of the rebels' bus, while his troops surrounded it. While one of the loyal soldiers was calling on the rebels to surrender, Second Lieutenant Bolanos Chavez was grasped from behind by a rebel officer who had descended and both bands began to fire. The rebels were routed and fled to the hills. Lieutenant Bolanos Chavez and two men were wounded. One loyal soldier was killed.

The balance of the contingent of riflemen under the command of Major Chupina Barahona conducted a fruitless raking operation in the area without making contact with the enemy, and then continued to Zacapa.

The rebel guerrillas retreated and the leader, Yon Sosa, escaped.

This was the heroic action that Jacobo Arbenz had hailed over Radio Havana as the beginning of guerrilla war in Guatemala.

III

At nine on January 24, 1962, a few days before the guerrilla skirmishes took place, the chief of the judicial police, Ranulfo

Gonzalez Ovalle, stepped from his home in Guatemala City into the street and got into his car. At the very moment that the driver started the motor, while Gonzalez Ovalle and his aide accommodated themselves in the back seat, a car drew up alongside and two machine guns simultaneously loosed a thunderous barrage of death. Gonzalez Ovalle was killed instantly, receiving seven shots in his face and body. The driver was wounded but by some miracle the chief's aide was unharmed. Gonzalez Ovalle was thirty-seven years old; he had been in charge of the judicial police for a short time.

The last document drawn up by Gonzalez Ovalle was memorandum number 563 to the President of the Republic, dated January 23, the day before he was killed. It bears his signature.

His report is chiefly a transcription of the declarations of one of four prisoners taken on the morning of January 23, 1962, the day before his death. This man, Carlos Calito Pineda, was a mechanic; he admitted being a member of the PGT and of the Partido de Unidad Revolucionario, PUR. He confessed that he had been one of the members of the Communist cell of zone three of Guatemala City, and that his two fellow members, two brothers, one, a lieutenant in the Guatemalan Army, were both in the Mexican Embassy under political asylum. Their names were Lieutenant Marco Tulio Contreras and Guillermo Eduardo Contreras. Calito Pineda said that he had been expelled from the Party because he had been suspected of being a government informer, and thus his cell was inoperative.

On the 9th of January, Calito Pineda had been approached by one Ruben Castellanos, a former employee of the supply department of the municipality of Guatemala City, and asked if he wanted to distribute subversive propaganda for the FIN (National Insurrectionist Front), banner under which the guerrilla rebels were combatting. He was offered $3.00 per day for his efforts. He confessed that he had dedicated himself to this work during four consecutive days. He then named four other individuals who had done the same. In his report Gonzalez Ovalle reported that the other propagandists were being sought. Calito Pineda declared that the movement was financed and directed by the leader of the Partido Revolucionario, Mario Mendez Montenegro, and other known politicians, whom I do not care to mention here, because they are still free in Guatemala.

Gonzalez Ovalle said that his investigations led him to believe that the terrorist bombs which daily plagued Guatemala at this time were the work of a group of Castro sympathizers, who had taken part in the November 13, 1960 uprising, and who were under the leadership of a major of the Guatemalan Army, named Prera.

He reported that a former minister and ambassador of my administration, who had as accomplices a colonel in charge of a military base in Guatemala, were also implicated. He reported that the recruiting center for this movement was located in Guatemala City and he gave me the exact address. He further stated that delegates were traveling to the interior of the country and forming cells for a peasant movement with the initials, CUCU (Committee for the Union of Peasants and Workers).

At the same time, he reported Marco Antonio Yon Sosa was operating in the Izabal, Zacapa and Chiquimula sectors. He said that Yon Sosa himself had been in the capital on the 20th, three days earlier, and that he had visited the headquarters of one of the revolutionary parties and urged them to support his movement to overthrow the government.

Gonzalez Ovalle further stated that a number of men who had taken part in the November 13, 1960 movement were meeting in the home of Major Prera. He said that troops were being sent to the northern sector of the country (where the outbreak actually occurred) in preparation for an attack on the military base at Zacapa. Yon Sosa was identified as being behind these activities.

Among the Communist propaganda, leaflets, handbills,

taken from Calito Pineda and the others, was a goodly supply of *The Shark and the Sardines,* by Juan José Arévelo.

Gonzalez Ovalle ended his report promising to diligently continue his endeavors and to keep me informed.

Twenty-four hours later he was dead.

IV

Beginning January 27, 1962, Guatemala was submitted to an outburst of terrorist bombings. A police post in the outskirts of the city received a rain of machine gun fire from a car that sped by in the dark.

On the 3rd of February a bomb exploded in the archive room of the Supreme Court, where inscriptions of notaries were kept. At almost the same moment, another bomb exploded in the interior of a Catholic church in the center of the city. Two days later, another bomb exploded in the vicinity of the National University, at the very moment that the university students were voting for a rector of the university.

Simultaneously, we saw the first symptoms of a student strike and protests began to be aired regarding the results of Congressional elections that had been consummated two months earlier, in December of the previous year. In these events, we foresaw the course of the expected action, promised by Dorticos in Montevideo, announced by Arbenz from Havana, and confirmed in the already familiar symptoms of a "National Liberation Movement."

On the 11th of February, a man was apprehended in Guatemala City who was transporting a small arsenal in his automobile; he had a sawed-off shotgun, a Reissing .45 sub-machine gun; two 9MM Matzen submachine guns, two hand grenades, and a good quantity of ammunition for the arms. On the same night, in another place, we found 143 Molotov cocktails, another sawed-off shotgun, and other explosives.

On the 16th the train from Puerto Barrios to Guatemala was derailed by removing a complete rail. The locomotive and three cars were upset.

Telegraph and telephone lines were cut on the night of the 20th and a tremendous conflagration was produced when incendiaries set fire to the national park, El Filon, in the outskirts of Guatemala City.

On the same night, judicial police found a handbill that called for the following:

1. Painting the number "13" on streets and houses (for the November 13, 1960 Movement).

2. Dedication of musical selections in honor of the rebels in programs on commercial radio stations.

3. A whispering campaign to favor the rebels.

4. Attacks on the military and their families.

5. Collection of funds, medicines and supplies for the guerrillas.

6. All kinds of agitation, street demonstrations and riots.

7. Sabotage of automobiles in the streets.

8. Sabotage of telephone, telegraph and electric lines. Renewed sabotage of the railroad.

On the afternoon of February 20, Roberto Montenegro Gonzalez, known to be the second in command of the FIN movement, took asylum in the Mexican Embassy.

On the night of February 21, nearly 300 convicts, under the effect of drugs which had been smuggled into the penitentiary, created a riot; they were almost able to overpower the guards and to dominate the prison.

On the night of the 26th of February, seven terrorist bombs exploded and a commercial radio station was assaulted by three masked bandits who obliged the operator to transmit a taped subversive message.

On the first of March, one hundred university students, all dressed in strict mourning, paraded through the streets toward the National Congress, arriving at the doors of the legislative body at 10:35 A.M., where they deposited an

enormous wreath. The parade was led by the directors of the
AEU (Association of University Students) and the president
of the organization, a known Communist, and student leader,
Arnulfo Parada Tobar, who made a speech explaining that
the act was a protest by the student organization against the
convening of a fraudulently elected congress and asked that
a moment of silence be observed for the "death of legality in
Guatemala." The students disbanded without being in any
way molested by the authorities.

V

By March Congress had already been inaugurated and the
congressmen had taken their seats. These elections of 1961
had given my party eleven seats out of thirty-three that were
being contested.

The Guatemalan Congress is made up of sixty-six seats,
50 per cent of which are renewed annually. Twenty-two opposition congressmen had been elected, strengthening the
ranks of the rightest and leftist extremists. However, I had
succeeded in obtaining a majority, however slight, in the
National Congress. My enemies of the Right and Left knew
that I would push passage of the reform laws that the economy
and social organization of the country were crying for des-
perately and which I had been trying to legislate for three
years. My majority had wrested control from the opposition
over the legislative body, and, from the clamor anyone would
have believed that it was my intention to recommend laws
that would return Guatemala to the Dark Ages. Indeed, it
would seem that this opinion prevailed in the United States
from the tenor of the reports that were printed on Guatemala.

All the opposition parties had presented claims for fraud,
malpractice or other accusations, to annul the elections for
seats they had lost. In the departments where they won
neither the revolutionary parties nor any others made mention
of fraud or malpractice. They calmly took their seats.

In the United States few know or understand what a Latin American university student organization represents. Our systems of higher education are completely different. In Guatemala a student may matriculate in any one of the ten faculties of the National University and he may submit himself to examination on any given subject twenty or thirty times, until at last he gives up in boredom or dies of old age, or passes. The examination is given by commissions who interrogate the student personally on the subject. These are all faculty members. The faculty itself is nominated by the students and may be reproved by the students. The students have an active voice in the administration of the university. Such a situation is incomprehensible in countries where students are disciplined and go to college to learn, not to teach the faculty how to proceed. The student organization in Guatemala is heavily infiltrated with Communists, and although these are in a minority they are capable politicians and control the organization.

The loose system of study has created a corps of veterans, "eternal students," who have very little inclination to finish their studies but who take the leadership in student politics. These are in a majority in the Law Faculty. And it is here that the Communists make easy conquests. It is thus that these eternal students find a way of life. The democratic institutions of the nation and of the world have no need of these persons, so they can sell their services only to the Communist Party.

The Constitution of Guatemala provides that the University of San Carlos (the National University, founded during the colonial period) is autonomous, that it must receive a yearly subsidy of no less than 2 per cent of the total national budget, that it has the exclusive right to license the practice of all professions, and is the arbiter for the incorporation of foreign professionals to practice in Guatemala. The university is governed by the Supreme University Council, which is self-perpetuating, which is made up of the university authorities and faculty, and representatives of the professional colleges and the student body.

But the students have another resource besides the direct administration of university affairs through participation in the Supreme Council. This is in the student associations themselves, of which there is one central association, the AEU, whose component elements are the student associations of each faculty—Law, Economics, Medicine, etc. The central student association, of course, controls the participation of the students in the Supreme University Council. The chief activity of the AEU is national politics.

When the moment comes for the elections of the officers of the different student associations, the true students, those who do not want to fall behind in their studies and who have no intention of making a career of "studying," leave politics in the hands of the "eternal students." These hold the elections at burdensome hours, drag the meetings out endlessly, and use all the ruses so well known in the United States to be the tools of unscrupulous labor leaders to control elections in their unions. As a matter of course, the elections are won by the "politicians."

Some of the more truly civic-minded students participate in the elections and make an effort to win them. But as of March 1962, the Guatemala University Student Association was dominated by Communist sympathizers. Since then, there have been changes in some of the student organizations as a result of the very flagrant and abusive attitudes of the student leaders. The Guatemalan university student receives free education. There are certain matriculation, examination, and laboratory fees, but in Guatemala, anyone who has finished his secondary education may matriculate in the faculty he desires and pursue his studies, day or night, without paying a cent for tuition. Further, it has long been a practice for the government to employ students of medicine, law, engineering, and students of other faculties in the administration, in whatever branch of government corresponds to the studies undertaken. Moreover, numerous engineering students are employed in the Communications Ministry (roads and public works), and these are allowed special working hours to permit them to attend classes.

The clerks in all of the lower courts of Guatemala are law students. This circumstance, the employment of law students in the lower courts, gives them multiple opportunities to place obstacles in the legal development of judicial procedure. I have already mentioned how suspects of acts of subversion or terrorism were readily released, to the consternation of the military and police authorities, and to my own frustration. But the fact is that the magistrates are usually members of the Law Faculty, and an important percentage of their income is obtained from this well-remunerated teaching activity (more than as magistrates). Consequently, they fear to contradict the students because they may lose their faculty seats through student pressure.

A flagrant case which clearly demonstrates the power of the students occurred when the Supreme University Council voted to demand that I resign as President of Guatemala. José Garcia Bauer, brother of Carlos Garcia Bauer, whose brilliant refutation of Cuba's Osvaldo Dorticos at Punta del Este made history, objected and voted against the measure. For this he was expelled from the Law Faculty of the University of San Carlos where he had served honorably and efficiently for many years.

This control of the lower courts by the Communists, through the subversive students, is maddening. The Terrorist Repression Law in Guatemala forbids the release under bail of persons indicted for crimes of treason; however, the clerks merely alter the charges and the suspects go free. That is why so many persons whose names are mentioned in this book are today walking the streets of Guatemala as free men. Although we make hundreds of arrests, most agitators are released before they can even be properly questioned.

Colonel Gildardo Monzon, one of my closest and most

trusted colleagues, who has stood beside me in every crisis, occupied the post of Minister of the Interior provisionally. He sent a memorandum to the Supreme Court asking for an opinion on the control of the lower courts by the students. "This is true," the magistrates replied. "We can remove judges, but we have no jurisdiction over the employees of the courts. These are the exclusive jurisdiction of the magistrate himself."

What can be done? In a constitutional republic the only path is legislation. Were I to ignore or by-pass the laws, I would do Guatemala lasting harm.

VI

The turbulence was rising like a storm on the horizon. The Communists saw major defeat written in the 1962 Congress where measures for the good of all were to be approved.

It was for this reason that every effort was made to keep Congress from convening, and when that was impossible to disrupt the entire nation.

The Association of University Students (AEU) hurled an ultimatum at me: disband Congress, declare the elections illegal and convoke new congressional elections, or face the consequences! If I had wanted a formula to destroy the constitutional life of Guatemala, here was the perfect one. Using as a protest the accusation that my administration was illegal, the university students demanded that I disregard every law of the country. Only in absolute dictatorships could such measures as they demanded be carried out. I, of course, replied in the negative, pointing out their error.

The reply to my refusal to consider their demands was an immediate strike among the university students, and their loyal ranks in the courts of justice in the nation. Neither the university nor the law courts functioned from that day.

The secondary school students' association, FUEGO, demonstrated on March 2 before the British Embassy. A student was held prisoner by the British authorities in Belize, and the students held a meeting in the Central Plaza after marching before the British Embassy.

Guatemala City became the scene of violence on March 9, and this situation continued for some time. Secondary school and university students, enrolled in the cause and urged on and led by known Communists, roamed through the streets armed with clubs, stones and sticks, and set themselves to disrupting traffic, threatening pedestrians, damaging private property, and admonishing merchants to close their stores.

Students of both sexes faithfully carried out the orders received from their leaders. The streets were littered with pieces of cardboard pierced by tacks that punctured automobile tires. So well indoctrinated were the youngsters that a little tot, who could not have been more than ten years old, approached a reporter on the staff of *El Imparcial* and said: "Are you a newspaperman? Then take note of what I am going to say. Our movement is a nationalist movement, idealist, we are against administrative corruption and fraudulent elections. We have the right to demonstrate, our movement is constitutional and juridic . . ."

On this day I did as I had done on other occasions, I went into the streets to show myself and to personally take the pulse of the public. At the corner of Sixth Avenue and 11th Street, a young man shouted insults at me from a bus. I motioned to the driver to stop and to the amazement of everyone I climbed into the bus. I looked around at the silent passengers, and especially at the face of a young boy who glowered at me. I took him by the hand and invited him to get off the bus. He resisted, fearing some reprisal, but I assured him that nothing would happen, that all I wanted to do was to talk to him.

"You are the one who shouted at me? What do you want?" He was dumb with fright and pale as a sheet. I noticed something extraordinary about his appearance, there was a bulge at his waist, a suspicious bulge. I opened his little jacket, and stuck into his belt was a .22-calibre automatic pistol. Without a word, I took it from him and handed it to my assistant. Instead of having the youngster arrested for the illegal possession of arms, for carrying concealed weapons, for insulting the President, and for threatening the President while in the possession of arms, all I did was make him walk a few steps with me.

The young man refused to talk. When he calmed down, I motioned him gently away. "Go home," I said. "And keep out of mischief."

Guatemalan newspaperman Isidoro Zarco had the courage to write an article calling the people to order and protesting the disorders. On the night of the 12th of March, he was rewarded with a potent bomb in his front yard. Fortunately there were no fatalities.

That day was the first of a week of violent disorders. The students erected barricades in the street to stop traffic. While some held their ground, others formed marauding patrols which terrorized the center of the city. The chief disorders were in the neighborhood of the Law Faculty and two secondary schools for boys. The police were obliged to intervene with tear bombs. They suffered hundreds of wounds from stones and blows, and more than one had to be hospitalized and others suffered permanent damage to their eyes, ears, and other delicate organs. What could we do? Machinegun unarmed youths? This was precisely what the subversive adults behind the matter wanted us to do. I gave strict orders that extreme caution was to be exercised to avoid fatalities. Hundreds were arrested, but quickly released.

It is impossible to give a blow-by-blow account of this uprising; space does not permit. The disorders reached their height on March 16, after telephone, telegraph and electric installations were scientifically sabotaged. The agitators had infiltrated every civic organization and labor union.

The leaders of the student movement soon identified themselves beyond a doubt, and all had interesting records in the files of our judicial police:

Arnulfo Parada Tobar, principal leader of the AEU, had three trips behind the Iron Curtain to his credit.

Luis Castillo Ralda had made three trips to Cuba, and was accused of firing on his companion in order to place the blame on the police.

Carlos Ernest Rojas, law student, had traveled to Cuba four times and was accused of smuggling money into Guatemala and distributing it for subversive purposes.

On the 16th of March the banks were unable to open, all the schools were on strike, the railroads were paralyzed, the city was a theatre of violence and agitation; indeed, at this moment, the subversives must have believed that victory was theirs. Who, witnessing such a state of affairs, could fail to believe me doomed?

On that day, the following cablegram, addressed to the Association of University Students, was received by the international communications office, which had been placed under strict supervision:

GU 728 FC 2539 VC 305 PEKING 204/101 16 19 39

NLT Asociacion Universitarios de Guatemala
10a Avenida "A" 5-40, Zona 1, Guatemala

LEARNING GUATEMALAN REACTIONARY AUTHORITIES FRENZIED SUPPRESSION ILLEGAL ARREST OF STUDENTS ENGAGED IN JUST STRUGGLE AGAINST REACTIONARY INTERNAL EXTERNAL POLICIES YDIGORAS DICTATORSHIP CHINESE STUDENTS EXPRESS IMMENSE INDIGNATION STRONG CONDEMNATION AND VOICE RESOLUTE SUPPORT FOR GUATEMALAN STUDENTS JUST STRUGGLE STOP NO SUPPRESSIVE MEASURES WHATSOEVER WILL SAVE UNITED STATES IMPERIALISM AND ITS LACKEYS FROM DOOM BUT WILL ONLY AROUSE ANGER AMONG GUATEMALAN PEOPLE STUDENTS FIGHT FOR NATIONAL LIBERATION STOP WE ARE DEEPLY CONVINCED FINAL VICTORY WILL SURELY BELONG GUATEMALA PEOPLE STUDENTS INASMUCH AS THEY FIGHT PERSISTENTLY.

ALL CHINA STUDENTS FEDERATION

The original of this cablegram was in English.

A radio monitor reported that radio Havana on the night of the 17th of March carried a message to the people of Guatemala in the voice of Jacobo Arbenz exhorting all Guatemalans to continue their struggle against my government. Arbenz is reported chiding the laborers and peasants who did not rise up to place themselves at the sides of the subversives for being "cowards." This same monitor reported that the program contained a taped message in the voice of Fidel Castro himself:

We have the support of powerful forces to give triumph to the Guatemalan revolution. It will be you, the peasants and workers, who will in reality impose your will on Guatemala and create, without a doubt, another socialist republic, such as China, such as Cuba, that will defend your rights against Yankee imperialism. You can depend—not only on the support of Cuba—but also on all the socialist nations of the world who are willing to cooperate with free nations such as Guatemala, that live under the boot of North American imperialism, through the treachery of the puppet governments which you suffer.

Day after day the riots continued, new means of upsetting the normal course of events were found. The most ingenious was one put into effect on the night of March 28. A small group of youngsters hammered metal splinters into the locks of over sixty commercial establishments on Guatemala's Sixth Avenue. There were not sufficient locksmiths in all Guatemala to repair all these doors on the following day.

A technician of the electric light company declared that three successful sabotage operations against their lines "were exactly the same as those that took place in Cuba shortly before Castro came into power." He added that the sabotage of high tension lines such as these had to be done by experts and that in all the history of the company such methods had never before been seen in Guatemala.

VII

Guatemala suffered additional weeks of agitation. I could describe incident after incident. I do not think that, in the history of Central America, and perhaps all Latin America, a government has ever weathered such a siege as mine for so long. In neighboring El Salvador, the government of José Mariá Lemus was overthrown by a few incidents. It has been the history of Latin America for governments to succumb quickly, unless such movements were suppressed with wholesale massacres, mass arrests, and other forms of violent repression.

By the end of the first week of April the movement had lost impetus. The schools, university and certain labor unions maintained their strike. But people were becoming restive and it seemed that the end was in sight.

However, at this critical moment one of the most tragic incidents of my entire regime took place. Four university students were killed on April 12, 1962.

At six o'clock on the afternoon of April 12, a military patrol approached the National Congress to relieve the guards who stood at the entrance. The Congress is directly across the street from the Law Faculty, and of course this was the center of most of the agitation.

On this day, as the troops approached, some students attempted to disarm the men and grappled with the soldiers, trying to wrest their rifles from them. The guards fought back but did not use their weapons. When the skirmish was practically under control of the guards, an automobile crossed the intersecting corner and a pistol shot was heard. It was directed at the truck which had brought the patrol, and one of the guards was wounded. One of the men, within the vehicle, lost his head and began to fire his machine gun, intending to loose the shots into the air in order to frighten the attackers. However, when one of his companions lunged at him to take

the weapon from him, the street was sprayed with bullets, and
three students were killed. The soldier was immediately disarmed, but the harm was done.

One hour later, another student was killed by shots from
another (or perhaps the same) car, from the same intersection.
Both incidents were perfectly timed to cast fuel on a dying
fire.

On the following day, the 13th of April, the Supreme Council of the University resolved to request my resignation as
President of Guatemala. The municipality of Guatemala and
three of the opposition political parties—Democracia Cristiana, Partido Revolucionario and MLN—joined them. The
professionals of Guatemala, through their different associations, declared their solidarity with the strikers in requesting
my resignation. A new political movement had been incu-
bated. This was the coalition that the "national liberation
movement" strategy aimed at. Fortunately, the movement
against me was only skin deep, it did not reach the core of
Guatemala. It was the clamor of a faction and not the voice
of the people.

No president could have survived such a situation without
the support of the people. Only by the use of violent repres-
sions, mass arrests, and persecutions, such as used by Hitler,
Stalin, and Trujillo, could a President have weathered such
a situation if he did not have the support of the people.

If I had committed such crimes in order to remain in office,
mine would be a black name in the history of Latin America.
But I remained President because I did not resort to the ex-
pedients of dictators. There was not then nor has there ever
been a popular repudiation of my administration. If there had
been, I would not be writing this as President of Guatemala,
but as an exile.

If I had committed mass murders, mass imprisonments,
flagrant violations of the Constitution, and every illegal
measure used by tyrants and dictators to maintain themselves
in power against the will of the people, this would have been
made known to the world.

A truce was declared for Holy Week; there was no pact, no written agreement, but the idiosyncrasy of the Latin American was manifested by a relaxing of tension, cessation of terrorist bombings, no street demonstrations. However, the Communist leaders had left the capital to organize strikes elsewhere.

Up to that moment, the Catholic Church had taken little part in the movement; no condemnation had been issued from the Episcopate, nor calls to peace.

On Good Friday, the most important place in Guatemala is the Church of Santo Domingo, on Twelfth Avenue. From here the procession of the holy burial takes place, and it has been my custom to be one of the pallbearers since my youth and even as President I observed this custom. On that morning a Red flag with the hammer and sickle was found flying from the Monsignor's flagpole, placed there during the night by a subversive agent.

On the Monday after Easter, the Provincial Episcopate of Guatemala issued a pronouncement condemning the grave threat of atheistic, materialistic and totalitarian communism.

The Pastoral Letter was signed by the archbishop and twelve bishops, and was published in the daily papers at their expense.

Now, almost three months after the extreme agitation had begun, the clergy became alarmed and called on the people to avoid involvement with communism. It cautioned parents to discipline misguided children. It said that it was beyond the pale of their pastoral duties to mix in politics, but that they felt it was their duty to warn the people of this grave danger.

This pronouncement, although tardy, did much to remove doubts from the minds of many as to the true nature of the movement. It ordered Catholics to cooperate for reestablishment of order. The following is translated from the Pastoral Letter:

It is urgent that Catholics cooperate for the reestablishment of public order as a grave matter of conscience; but more so despite the existence of questions of local interest subject to personal interpretation, the audacity of the Communists is evident for all to see, and these can take advantage of non-Communists who support the movement for their own ends.

The story of these riots and disturbances would itself fill a book. I was obliged to change my cabinet and I placed one of my trusted officers as Minister of the Interior, Colonel Gildardo Monzon. His firm hand was immediately respected and, while incidents did not cease, the tension was eased slightly.

Violence ended, the various political parties began to talk. The most important meeting was held in the home of a distinguished and respected fellow citizen, who played no part in politics. Three ambassadors were present, those of El Salvador, Honduras and Venezuela. Three members from each of the political parties attended, including my own. Represented were the Partido Revolucionario, Democracia Cristiana, MLN, MDN and Redencíon.

The opposition had chosen as their spokesman, Dr. René de Leon Schloter, a congressman of the Democracia Cristiana Party. He stood up and said that he would make an analysis of all the enormous mistakes and enumerate the damage which Guatemala had suffered under the rule of General Ydígoras Fuentes. In a pathetic tone he described the trials of the peoples and the enormous number of new taxes that Ydígoras Fuentes had levied on his suffering people, behind their backs. He spoke for about twenty minutes.

Then I took the floor and said, "I am going to ask you one question, just one single question. Point out and demonstrate, name one single new tax that President Ydígoras Fuentes has imposed on Guatemala."

Dr. Schloter knit his brows, mumbled to himself, looked appealingly at his fellows, then muttered: "Well, the truth is there are no *new* taxes, but you *threaten* to impose them."

I then tore his argument to pieces, and when there was nothing more to be said about his unfounded statements we began to discuss the situation from a legal point of view. I sparred with half a dozen lawyers or more—most of them members of Congress—but they had to admit defeat, being unable to point to a single illegality in my administration. They could do nothing but give up. They had arrived proud and arrogant; they left humbled. Don Luis Beltranena, our host, declared before all the witnesses, including the three ambassadors, who were: Manuel Villeda Morales of Honduras; Lieutenant Colonel Miguel Alvaro Rivas of El Salvador; and Colonel Tomas Perez Tenreiro of Venezuela; that in all his life he had never heard a more historic debate nor witnessed a more crushing defeat, than that which I had inflicted on my political opponents.

They had a further and even more humiliating embarrassment. When they urged the student leaders to set aside their aggressive campaign, the students replied that they could not accept the "purely personal point of view and interests" of the Democracia Cristiana, Revolutionary and MLN parties for "solving the grave political situation that prevailed in the nation."

In other words, the Association of University Students considered itself above the political parties as interpreters of the national interest. They insisted on my resignation, and other measures. They ended their manifesto with these words:

> People of Guatemala! We make a final appeal to you. All should set aside every sectarian position or personal interest on the altar of accord and in the national interest. We will wage the final battle! Unfurl the banners and offer your naked breasts to the tyranny. Forward!

This, of course, was salt in the political opposition's wounds. They saw how they had been deceived and realized that they had been tools of the Communists who stood behind the students. All Guatemala understood this.

I had no remedy but to reorganize my entire cabinet, and as I did not want to imperil the lives of the civilians with these posts, I appointed a full military cabinet; retaining only Dr. Unda Murillo, who held his own with any warrior. It was thus that events began to slack off.

On this same day, the 27th of April, the non-Communist students of the Faculty of Engineering attempted to dissuade their fellows from supporting the strike, but they were threatened with death by the leaders. However, opposition to the movement began to grow. A group of teachers published a declaration in the daily papers accusing the FUMN of coercion and threats to oblige them to maintain the strike. On the first of May the Communists had their parade, even though it had been prohibited. As a result there was a riot when the parade was broken up with tear bombs. The entire day was given over to violence and sabotage, and there were many bombs that night.

On the following afternoon, two expert saboteurs plied their trade on the gasoline storage tanks of the Esso Oil Company in Guatemala City. At 5:05 P.M. a concussion hand grenade was thrown at the tank and exploded, ripping a great hole through which the gasoline flooded out. The gasoline was ignited by some burning substance thrown into the stream.

The flames rose into the sky and a great cloud of smoke hovered on the horizon. The lives of thousands were endangered and the entire neighborhood had to be evacuated. It is not a fashionable one. It seemed as if the earth had opened to allow the very flames of hell to lap over the face of our city.

It was next to impossible to establish responsibility for the criminal act. Prompt examination of the grounds revealed footprints that led the investigators to conclude that only two persons had been involved. Abandoned in the area from which the hand grenade had been thrown, were found two fully-loaded clips of bullets for a Matzen machine gun.

Controlling the conflagration and holding back its spread to a limited area was a superhuman struggle. For thirty-six hours the fire department, with the help of the military, battled the flames. These were finally extinguished by chemical mediums. Seven firemen were injured and the damages were estimated at $350,000.

This was not the end. Sabotage continued. But as the Spanish saying goes: No sickness can last for a hundred years, nor is there a body capable of resisting that long. At length, on May 8, 1962, after almost 100 days of turmoil, the general assembly of the AEU decided to approve lifting the strike and returning to classes.

By the 15th of May it could be said that it was all over. At no moment had the thought of surrender crossed my mind. As I had told the people of Guatemala: only an assassin's bullet or the due legal process of a free election, would bring me to relinquish the presidency.

12

"COMMUNIST THREAT"–
FACT OR FICTION?

I

In March of 1962 my general staff was informed that armed groups were operating in the area of the Indian village of Chuarrancho to the north of Guatemala City, in heavily wooded and rough terrain. Troops were dispatched and when they arrived they found that the Indian peasants were gathered to lend aid and to take part in the action against the guerrillas.

The guerrillas took positions in the hillsides, where they found ample protection in the uneven terrain and thick woods. They opened fire on the loyal troops with machine guns and rifles. The guerrillas had a decided advantage in their covered positions.

The battle lasted for almost three hours. During the final minutes, loyalist and rebel fought body to body. Our troops had received special training in anti-guerrilla tactics and here they proved their efficiency. The rebels were routed and fled abandoning arms, explosives, ammunition, supplies, medicines, and Communist propaganda.

On the 13th of April the university students published a list of their companions who had been killed in the guerrilla battles. The list gave the number of dead correctly as thirteen, two of whom were not identified. This list named *Juan Francisco Barrios de Leon* as one of the casualties.

On June 4 a Communist underground publication, *Verdad,* again mentioned the Garnados battle. This list named eleven persons and also placed *Juan Francisco Barrios de Leon* among the dead.

The case of Juan Francisco Barrios de Leon is interesting.

On the 22nd of November of the year before (1961), Guatemala City was moved by the disappearance of a young student. The newspaper, *Impacto,* carried the following lead on page 3 of that day:

DISAPPEARS ON HIS RETURN FROM MEXICO—
WHERE HE WAS STUDYING

Worried Mother Denounces the Detention of her Son by the Immigration Authorities—Who Deny the Act— For Which Writ of Habeas Corpus has been Presented.

The disappearance of her son, the young student, Juan Francisco Barrios, 27, was denounced yesterday to the editorial department of this newspaper by his mother, Teresa de Leon de Barrios, who says that although her son was captured by immigration guards at a place on the Mexican frontier called El Carmen on the 13th, he has not appeared . . . Senora de Leon de Barrios said that her son had left for Mexico on the 24th of February of this year to finish his studies and that he was returning to Guatemala to spend his vacation with his family.

El Imparcial on the same day said that the family of the young man had also visited their editorial offices and expressed concern for his personal safety.

On the 29th of November the "young student" was still among the missing. The association of law students, El Derecho, then published a statement announcing that the young man had been assassinated by the Guatemalan government. The student association gave the government twenty-four

hours to produce the "victim" in good health or be responsible
for a new "political assassination." This hue and cry was taken
up by the susceptible newspapers of Guatemala who published
articles portraying the government as cut-throats and me as
the chief assassin.

Then, on December 2, 1961, the front page of *El Imparcial*
carried a photograph of Juan Francisco Barrios de Leon who
had mysteriously come back to life.

Here are the facts behind the case: Francisco Barrios de
Leon was neither a university student nor a student of any
kind. He was a printer by profession and his connections with
communism went back to the days of Arbenz. He was twenty-
seven years old at the time of his death.

He was apprehended near the Mexican border and his
declarations to the authorities (copy of which is included in
the illustrative sections of this book) relate the following:

His older brother, Rosalio, was a school teacher and a member of the PGT (Guatemalan Communist Party, underground). Juan Francisco began to participate in the activities
of the party in 1953 when he became a member of the Youth
Alliance. When Arbenz resigned in 1954, he took refuge in
the Argentine Embassy and left Guatemala for that country,
where he remained for two years. He returned to Guatemala
in 1956 and until 1961, he said, he had no connections with
any political activities.

His protestations of being non-political are hard to believe
because on February 25, 1961, he suddenly goes to Mexico
where he immediately contacts members of the PGT; and
they readily arrange his transportation to Cuba, where he remains for approximately one month. From Cuba he is then
taken by air to Prague, where he remains for three days and
then to Moscow, where he remains another three days, and
from there to Peking, where he receives a course of indoctrination which covers several months.

He returned to Guatemala via Leningrad, Zochi, Stalingrad,

Prague, East Germany, Switzerland, Belgium, Canada and Mexico. From Mexico he proceeded overland to the Guatemalan border with two enormous suitcases. From the Mexican rail terminal he did not cross the border at the regular border crossing post, but continued north a few kilometers, perhaps on foot, and crossed at a point near a small town, El Carmen. He took the precaution of paying a smuggler to "pass" his luggage. All border towns have delegates from the immigration office and the one here stopped Barrios de Leon and asked for his documentation. For reasons that have never been definitely established, Barrios de Leon had a passport that did not bear the seal of the immigration department, nor was it signed by the head of the department, nor any other official. Subsequent investigation showed that he had filled in and signed an application for a passport in January of 1961. We presume that some accomplice in the department stole the travel document and gave it to him before the security check to which all passport applications are subjected was carried out. Presumably they foresaw difficulties in obtaining a passport for Barrios de Leon because of his Communist record. However, this was a fatal error, because Barrios de Leon would have been issued a passport, despite his record, and if he had not carried the illegal passport he would not have been detained. Everything else was in order except the suspicious manner in which he had entered Guatemala and his confusing and contradictory story. The immigration delegate became suspicious and he detained Barrios de Leon and wired his chiefs. Agents were immediately dispatched, and when his baggage was searched it was found to contain a veritable treasure trove of Communist propaganda, mementoes, and instructions.

The authorities found twenty-two handwritten blank-books with careful notes covering his entire training course. He had painstakingly typed out all the notes in duplicate. The typed pages totalled ninety-five legal-size sheets that had well over 500 words per page: 50,000 words of the most explosive literature. His studies seemed to have covered every facet of international communism from the constitution of the Communist Party to guerrilla warfare and demolition and sabotage tactics. If he had devoted his talents to legal activities there is no doubt that his patience, energy and perseverance would have carried him far. His work was more than sufficient to constitute a thesis for an advanced degree. His notes, transcribed from notebook number two, comprise a complete manual on demolition and sabotage, much more complete than "Che" Guevara's famous work. They contain formulas for preparing explosives, instructions for setting up chain explosions, the best method of destroying railroads, bridges, dams, walls, buildings; all in all, it is a remarkable "do it yourself" guerrilla handbook. It contains a complete study of the different types of arms used by modern infantry. His notes cover detailed instructions on the manufacture of land mines, bombs and hand grenades. The "young student" was indeed a dangerous man.

In the lining of his suitcase were found two military maps, one of Guatemala and the other of Guatemala City. These were carefully annotated and contained the military strategy intended to coincide with the political agitation that was being planned for six months later. We returned these maps to their hiding place after making photostats. This book is the first revelation to the rebels of our discovery of their plans.

Francisco Barrios de Leon was released and allowed to take the suitcase with the maps in the lining. All the propaganda, booklets, and indoctrination material were confiscated. He must have made immediate contact with his friends and allies, for the plans in his possession were later carried out to a great extent. But we were ready.

Thus, Francisco Barrios de Leon, "student leader," who was in reality a Communist agent, served to expose the connection between the supposedly "nationalist" movement in Guatemala and international communism. He gave his life for one cause but served another well.

II

On March 10, 1962, former President Juan José Arévalo, living in Mexico as a political exile, had lunch in the Chapultepec Restaurant with other Guatemalan émigrés, both military and civilian. Those present were Major Alfonso Prera, Lieutenant Jose G. Lavagnino, and Second Lieutenant Ruben Mendez.

The subject of conversation was the initiation of an armed movement against my government. Lavagnino disappeared from Mexico City five days later. On the 19th of March a group of ten men, wearing green uniforms, armed with machine guns, grenades and side arms, penetrated Guatemalan territory across the Mexican border in the Department of Huehuetenango. This party distinguished itself by taking reprisals against a humble Indian family that had refused to be impressed as porters. One of the men withdrew the firing pin from a grenade and stuck it into an empty tin can, handing it to a child. When he had rejoined the party, some 500 feet from the hut, the grenade exploded and as a result four were killed, including one infant.

These valiant guerrillas continued inland, meeting no resistance; however, their movements were reported and army troops were dispatched to deal with them. However, before the army contingents could arrive, the Indian population of San Mateo Ixtatan captured seven of the ten insurgents and the other three were soon trapped, captured, and tied in a nearby heavily wooded promontory. These were stripped naked and conducted to the town like roped animals. If the army contingents had not arrived soon after the capture of the guerrillas, it is possible that they would have been massacred by the indignant natives.

III

A document entitled, "For an evaluation of the battles of March"—dated March 27, 1962, and signed by the Political Committee of the Central Commission of the PGT—fell into our hands, as so often happens, through the disloyalty of one of the Communists.

The analysis runs to four closely typed pages and must contain well over 3,000 words, covering fourteen points. The first point candidly admits: "The Ydígoras government, once again, was able to weather the crisis. Never before has this government been nearer to collapse . . . ? The university and post-primary students are lauded for the 'courage and decision that was manifest in street fights and paralyzed traffic in the capital, responding to the strike decreed by the AEU.'

"Imperialist properties, such as the IRCA and the UFCO and reactionary elements, were made to feel the popular fury. Along with the popular warlike aggression, terrorist acts were carried out.

"The armed guerrilla movement did not play an important role in the recent crisis, nor could it yet, because it is just starting; nevertheless, it was the action of the 'Alejandro de Leon-13 de Noviembre' guerrilla front that in February created the first political tension in the country. During the crisis this front was able to carry out certain limited actions in the northeast of the country, and some of its adherents in the city joined the fight of the masses. In the north, the 'October 20' front, under the command of Colonel Carlos Paz Tejada, was intercepted by forces of the government and obliged to give battle.

"The sharpening of the crisis made it necessary to call for a general strike at a certain moment. Nevertheless, it must be confessed that the call met with no popular support and except for the events that paralyzed life in the capital for moments during the 13th, 14th, and 15th of March, it was not effective. The people certainly looked on our movement with sympathy, but they were not organized for a general strike. This calls not only for a high degree of conscience and decision, but also practical organization. Despite the significance of the strike of the SAMF (railroad workers' union), of the STIGGS (bank and employees of the Social Security Workers' Union) and of other unions, not enough work had been done to create conscience nor achieve the needed organization. And behind this failure, without a doubt, are found serious faults: lack of understanding of the moment, initiative, coordination, etc.

"If the work among the laborers was generally deficient, it must be pointed out that as far as the sectors of industry and commerce are concerned, even if it is true that they were against the government, their fear of a general popular outburst, their fear of the revolution, made them hesitate at each moment, caught 'between two waters,' and they did not respond to the call with decision. Only a few joined the movement at certain moments impelled by circumstances.

"The reactionary opposition, for its part, openly united and headed by the PR (Partido Revolucionario), sought a way out in the possible integration of a civic-military junta, that would to a large extent accept the demands of the AEU; but at the last moment, the movement did not jell, even though high ranking army officers were implicated.

"The chief factors that kept the Ydígoras government from being overthrown and bringing the present crisis to a head, were the following: a) the revolutionary forces are not yet capable of fully assuring the solution the country needs; b) the army, cracked and divided, and in a moment when it was inclined to oust Ydígoras, was afraid of the masses, and the possibility that revolutionary forces would achieve power, and preferred, for the moment, to maintain him. And it is obvious that the army was, at that moment, the only force capable of overthrowing the government; and c) conclusively, because North American imperialism, fearful that in the midst of the popular movement it could lose control of the situation, did not maneuver openly, although it had relations with the conspirators. Here the tendency of the North American imperialists to support as far as possible 'constitutional' governments, in order to preclude popular battles and violent changes from opening a pathway for the revolution, was manifest.

"But it is only just to point our own weaknesses and failings that once again were made evident: a) events were not used correctly to extend and cement our relations with the masses and thus win more and more candidates for membership in the party and the youth (movement); b) initiative, decision and daring were lacking in the battle; c) the distribution of propaganda was often slow, routine, and bureaucratic."

This document clearly illustrates the action of the Communist Party as the catalyst, or binding agent that unified the different forces within the country under the banner of the "national liberation" strategy. The use of the university students as the spearhead is clearly stated.

The usefulness of the opposition revolutionary parties, whom the Communists term "the reactionary opposition led by the Partido Revolucionario," is seen. Even the participation of United States forces, termed "North American imperialism," enters into their analysis. They mention the different labor unions, especially that of the rail workers (SAMF), and criticize these organizations for not having sufficient "conscience" and for being poorly organized.

After exploring all the negative aspects, the document takes a look at the future. Here it says: "The principal features and the prospects of the situation can be summed up in the following elements: a) a momentary resurgence back of the popular battle, where regroupings are taking place and where forces are being prepared; b) the political crisis may continue in the same decomposition . . . (illegible) . . . The conspiracy . . . (illegible) . . . with these elements the possibility of the substitution of Ydígoras by a coup inspired and supported by the Yankee Embassy or not, but in any event, limited, is also possible. And on the other hand, the renewal of the battle in violent shape has already been suggested.

"The strategy of the Party under these circumstances is to maintain the battle on every level in line with circumstances and to combine the different forms (of battle) in accord with the rising or falling (tempo) of the same; in conformity with its policy of political unification and of (uniting) the masses; to encourage the organization of the different popular sectors in every possible manner and to carry out a broad labor of uniting with the other forces and persons; to raise initiative and aggressiveness combativity; reinforce the work of the party in every field, recruiting, propaganda, etc.; and to take security measures in the face of the repression of the government forces. SECURITY AND BATTLE are now the two aspects of our battle."

IV

When I read such statements as: "Ydígoras governs for an illegitimate . . . profit"; "Ydígoras stole last year's elections"; "Ydígoras has used his office to make his son, Miguelito, and his Scottish son-in-law millionaires"; I am astonished and disillusioned. Strangely enough, the preceding remarks were not contained in a political commentary but in a review of a book[*] that gave my government objective and understanding treatment. (*Guatemala: The Story of an Emergent Latin American Democracy*, Mario Rosenthal; Twayne Publishers, New York; 1962. Reviewed in the *Saturday Review*, October 6, 1962.)

The reviewer was Harold Lavine, senior editor and Latin American correspondent of *Newsweek*.

Mr. Lavine's attacks on my government have not been limited to a book review.

---

[*]Mario Rosenthal, author of the book, *Guatemala: The Story of an Emergent Latin American Democracy*, wrote to the editors of the *Saturday Review* protesting the review, and refuting one statement made by Harold Lavine. Mr. Rosenthal's telling rebuttal was published in the Jan. 12, 1963 issue of the *Saturday Review*.

In a *Newsweek* report of April 2, 1962, Mr. Lavine characteristically said: "Ydígoras, characteristically, accused Fidel Castro of fomenting the student uprising. The facts were dead against him."

It is because of uninformed statements such as this that I have written this book.

I cite the following documents:

1) A letter from the Cuban "Crusade of Liberty" organization, dated January 16, 1962, directed to Rafael Solis Barrios, in Mexico. I will quote briefly from the letter:

> You must instruct the G-2 of the Guatemalan section, so that without delay we may discover the leak in the university and professional groups that we have been suffering in the recent past. It is not possible that the nefarious government that has usurped power in Guatemala be so well informed of the movements and traffic between this capital and that. The latest denunciations, that appeared in the newspapers, and which brought our student companions in Quezaltenango into the limelight, is the best evidence that there is a government agent infiltrated in our ranks and this is sufficient to threaten our security.
>
> Send us all kinds of information on the military base of Santa Elisa, which lies between Poptun and Coban. This is urgent and can be taken advantage of at Punta del Este if you send us proof in the sense that this is a military base set up by Ydígoras to invade Belize. In this way the English will increase their assistance to the traitorous and retrograde forces of the Liberation which will in the long run be to our benefit.

2) Letter from Havana dated March 16, 1962 directed to José Luis Hernandez at Quezaltenango, Guatemala. From which I quote:

> I am sending you this by means of Claude who is taking you $7,000 to be delivered through personal contact to your companion professors and students . . . It doesn't matter that members of the Liberation and Catholics are

infiltrating the movement. I repeat again that the end justifies the means and all of these will be purged afterwards . . . Besides the larks [undoubtedly planes] and the tunny [undoubtedly submarines] will arrive soon . . . Prepare lists of persons of counter-revolutionaries and worms, especially of the treasonous and bad sons of Marti . . . prepare lists of persons of known militancy in our cause to make up people's courts . . .

This letter also calls for immediate action in sabotage activities and names the objectives: bridges, aqueducts, telephones, electric light plants, stores, television and radio stations, and urban and interurban transportation. The letter mentions the broadcasts of Colonel Arbenz from Havana and urges that these programs be publicized as much as possible, and it contains a list of how the $7,000 is to be distributed.

3) On July 26, 1962 *La Prensa Libre* of Guatemala City published the following manifesto on page 32:

PRONOUNCEMENT OF THE ASSOCIATIONS OF STUDENTS OF LAW, HUMANITIES AND ECONOMY IN RELATION TO THE SIGNIFICANCE OF THE 26TH OF JULY.

The Cuban Revolution, dating from July 26, 1952, demonstrates objectively through actual events that under financial capitalism it is no longer possible to develop economically and socially. . . .

The Cuban Revolution has come to demonstrate that the only worthy path that leads to our total political and economic independence, is that which frees the peoples from the basic yoke: foreign investments around which all the other privileged classes turn.

We have awakened from an old lethargy . . . in a world split into two qualitatively different camps . . . the validity and effectiveness of local wars has expired, and today, it becomes dangerous to play with fire. That means that the sulphates can no longer plunder and exploit with impunity the sovereignty of peoples. Today there is a means of calling to order those who have lost their reason, our peoples, in their anxiety for independence, are no longer alone.

Guatemala, July 25, 1962

for the Association of Humanities
Carlos A. Figueroa
President

for the Association El Derecho
Libo Haroldo Gonzalez
Acting President

for the Association of Economics
Jaime F. Pineda S.
President

What can be added to this clear statement of solidarity with the Cuban Revolution and with the principles and aspirations of international communism?

The student organizations of the Law, Humanities and Economic Faculties in this declaration also told the people of Guatemala that there was no longer such a thing as a "local" war; that all conflicts are of an "international" nature. That the "sulphates" (the "corrosive acid of capitalism") can no longer plunder and exploit with impunity because a means of calling to order those who have lost their reason; "our peoples, in their anxiety for independence, *are no longer alone.*"

It is indeed curious that critics of my "iron-handed rule" have not found the opportunity to comment on the fact that a) Guatemalan students could freely prepare such a manifesto as I quote from above; b) they were able to meet to draw up such a document; c) Guatemalan newspapers were able to publish it with absolute impunity.

VII

Another significant symptom of the intervention of international communism in Guatemala was the attendance of Guatemalan students at the Eighth Helsinki World Youth Festival, which, as everyone knows, was sponsored by the

Kremlin. It is said that the Soviet invested over $104,000,000 in transportation and expenses to carry thousands of students from all over the world to Helsinki.

As the reader can see from copies of *Airline Passenger Manifests* reproduced on page 141, literally hordes of youngsters from all the countries of Latin America, including Guatemalans, were transported from Mexico to Cuba and thence to Europe to attend the festival. Also reproduced in these pages is a photostat of the ticket and travel document issued to student leader Julio Ibarra Mazarriegos. Thousands of postcards and letters were sent from Helsinki to friends and relatives in Guatemala; some of these are also reproduced. The passenger manifests clearly state that the transportation is "courtesy" or free, and many of these are for account of the ICAP (Cuban Institute for Friendship of Peoples) and even give the names of the hotels where the "tourists" will be accommodated in Havana for account of their hosts.

In short, this entire spectacle was no more than a Communist move to accelerate its propaganda and activities in the free world, particularly in Latin America. It is disheartening to see photographs of mere children, such as those reproduced in these pages, who attended the festival, and innocently displayed their native costumes for the amusement of their "comrades."

VIII

The most important event of 1962 was the decision of President Kennedy to impose an embargo on the shipment of arms to Cuba and to demand that its missile bases be dismantled.

Guatemala had officially advised the United States government of the rapidly mounting threat of aggression from Cuba, and of the existence of the Soviet bases.

We have a well-organized espionage system in Cuba. It is sometimes disrupted by the capture of some agent but it always gets back into operation. Through this source of operations we were able to confirm the existence of three types of missile platforms, four different types of rockets, fields for long distance and jet planes, and submarine bases and underground submarine shelters on the Cuban coasts.

At four o'clock on the afternoon of October 16, 1962, six days before President Kennedy declared the embargo, the United States Ambassador, John O. Bell, and Colonel Norman W. Geron, Chief of the United States Military Mission to Guatemala, came to my office, and conferred with Foreign Minister Jésus Unda Murillo and myself.

I informed my visitors that I had sufficient evidence to be convinced that there were nuclear weapons in Cuba, placed there by Russia.

I then offered the United States the use of locations on Guatemalan soil for the installation of missile sites and military bases. My gesture in offering these bases to the United States was not only to permit that country to defend itself against a possible aggression, but also to defend Central America and Guatemala from the same threat.

There was no exchange of notes or a written report of this meeting. However, pursuant to our commitments with the Organization of American States, the Guatemalan Ambassador to that Organization, Dr. Carlos Urrutia Aparicio, directed a memorandum to the president of the council, dated October 25, 1962, informing him of the conference.

British Foreign Secretary Lord Home succinctly expressed the feelings of intelligent democrats everywhere in the world on the Cuban crisis when he said, in defense of the United States policy:

This was, then, not a question of American policy towards Cuba, but a question of Communist policy toward the free world. We do not have to say "I am for America, right or wrong," what we have to do is to recognize that the basic Communist purposes of imposing their system on the rest of the world are consistent and relentless and that our safety and our freedom depend primarily on American power and American strength. If America is threatened, we are threatened. If America were to give way, Russia would be free to make life unpleasant for the rest of us . . . When Russia does things she has no business to do, the time to stop her is at the beginning.

IX

Toward the middle of November, I received word of renewed anti-Guatemalan activity in Cuba, and I threatened to recognize a Cuban government in exile if Castro did not stop supporting former President Jacobo Arbenz.

On November 14, 1962, the Mexican newspaper *Atisbos* commented editorially on this as follows:

"Arbenz has the intention, with the interventionist support of Castro, of imposing on Guatemala a Red dictatorship, and since a legitimate government will not turn power over to the usurper on a silver platter, Arbenz will have to take course to violence, both from the exterior and to inspire internal subversion . . . Arbenz daily incites the people to rebellion over Radio Havana, and his partisans obtain arms to foment the revolution against Ydígoras. We do not doubt that the establishment of a government in exile would bring more troubles to Guatemala and exacerbate the hatred of international communism, but at least the Cuban patriots who fight for the liberation of their country will have a point of support and factor for unity. Guatemala does well in defending itself."

On the night of the 23rd of October, 1962, the Guatemalan Congress finally approved the Income Tax Law, which had been under study since 1959. This was achieved in a historic seventy-two hour session and after much opposition. This was the last link needed for Guatemala to qualify to participate in the program of the Alliance for Progress. The bi-lateral Guatemalan-United States agreement guaranteeing United States' investments in Guatemala against freezing and expropriation had been approved in September (this agreement had been followed by protest demonstrations against "Yankee imperialism") by the university students.

What followed the approval of the Income Tax Law was far more extreme.

I had known that both civilians and military were again plotting an uprising. The first word we had of this came from Cuba. We were informed that money was being sent to Guatemala, via Mexico and Panama, to buy the consciences of Guatemalans. We learned that a former student leader, Arnulfo Tobar, had brought the very sizable amount of $300,000 to Guatemala to finance the movement. We learned that Colonel Gonzalez Batres, a member of the air force, but who was too old to fly, had been bought off. The Minister of Defense called him to his office, since he still held his rank, and warned him that he was playing a dangerous game. The defecting Colonel replied that he had five legitimate children and eleven illegitimate children and that since he did not have enough money to support three households, he was naturally disgruntled. Instead of clapping the cynical Colonel in jail, the Minister of Defense dispatched him out of the country on a scholarship, and provided him with extra wages to meet his obligations.

Another army man won over by Castro gold was Colonel Oscar Giron Perrone, assistant director of the Military Hospital of Guatemala City. He promoted the movement and held secret meetings inside the hospital, attended by men who were known to be pro-Communist. His own friends informed the government that he was drawing checks against the Bank of America in Guatemala City for unusual amounts, far in excess of his wages. The matter was investigated and we found that he was extending checks to "bearer" for wine, women and song. He was dismissed from the army but he continued to distribute money to win over followers. Letters directed to

him from Cuba via Mexico were intercepted, and from these
we learned that not only were several members of the underground Communist Party, the PGT, involved in the matter,
but also those of other leftist organizations.

Also many people of comfortable economic positions were
unhappy; because in Guatemala, during its entire 141 years
of independence, they and their families had never paid one
cent in income tax. They now saw a threat in the laws that
reformed the tenure of property in Guatemala and the holding
of fallow lands and, of course, the Income Tax Law.

The activities of the different groups shaped up into a
conspiracy, and some semblance of unity was reached. I have
the idea that these conspiratorial organizations are somewhat
like furunculitis (boils) in that if they do not come to a
head, the germ remains latent within the body. We can
compare the different attempts of Castro-communism against
Guatemala to attacks of this disease, and with each eruption
we have brought some of the poison to a head and cut it from
the body of the nation.

We can also compare these conspiratorial activities in
Central America and all of Latin America, with our volcanoes.
We have thirty-two volcanoes in Guatemala and there are
always two or three in active eruption. We like to see these
volcanoes spew flames and ash and lava, because these harm-
less eruptions produce lava, ash and sand, and much smoke
and mountains of gases. This keeps the country from suffering
disastrous earthquakes, and the ashes serve to enrich our soil.

At nine A.M., November 25, I had a meeting in my official
residence, Casa Crema, with the Minister of Defense, the
Minister of the Interior, and the Minister of Labor, and
their aides. Strange as it may seem, we were virtually waiting
for an explosion.

As I sat in my office, on this Sunday morning, with my
ministers and aides, our ears were assailed by the whine of
airplane engines diving at the ground, and the deafening
explosion of .50-calibre machine gun fire, rockets and bombs.

Minutes earlier the plotters, both civilian and military plotters, had converged on the La Aurora Air Force Base, and it had been captured with the help of those who had been won over to their cause within the base. Several P-51 planes had been quickly dispatched with their eight .50-calibre machine guns, eight rockets, and 100- and 200-pound bombs, and told to blow my residence off the face of the earth.

A shower of bullets and rockets fell at the very door of my office, where I was discussing the situation with my ministers. I picked up the direct wire telephone with the air force base. The commandant of the base, Colonel José Luis Lemus, answered. I asked him to identify the attacking planes. He was only able to reply in frenzied voice, "The air force has rebelled." Then we were cut off.

My immediate reaction was to telephone the other army bases and to alert them to the danger so that they could take every precaution to defend their personnel and installations. Anti-aircraft machine guns were carried to the roof of Casa Crema and a small defense corps was organized. I sent my wife and grandchildren away. My devoted wife did not want to leave my side, and I had to virtually place her under arrest to see that she was taken to a place of safety.

A quick inspection of my residence revealed that bullets had fallen across the very beds of my grandchildren, in my bedroom, and in the corridors.

The intention of the attack was evident; I was to be assassinated.

I took up a light machine gun and I slung it around my shoulder and followed by my close aides, I went out into the street to take personal command of the presidential guard of honor, three blocks from my residence. While we were in the streets a new air attack was loosed on Casa Crema with .50-calibre projectiles and rockets. The explosion was ear-splitting, but we continued. The P-51 saw us and swept down and loosed a hail of lead around us.

One of the soldiers who was at my side was wounded, and I was pulled to the ground by Lieutenant Mario R. Espana, who refused to let me up until the second attack was over. I was indignant, of course, but quickly realized that in all probability the loyal Lieutenant had saved my life, for I was so infuriated that I was paying no heed whatsoever to the rain of bullets.

We reached the headquarters of the guard of honor and found everything calm. Outside, anti-aircraft cannon and machine guns were firing from the rooftops; the barracks had already suffered one attack and at the very moment that we gained cover a cluster of five P-51's dove at us and loosed rockets, bombs and machine gun fire in such quantity that the very earth shook.

I was very impressed by the fact that our infantry was not in the least afraid of air attacks, and this was due to the intense training they had been receiving during the past few years. The officers showed no signs of nervousness either, and they were as serene as if they had been participating in training maneuvers. The military commander of the brigade, with a coolness worthy of mention, calmly set about taking the first steps for "Operation Whip."

Meanwhile, the violent attacks from the air continued and we heard bullets and rockets whistling down on the barracks from all sides. "Operation Whip" began to function according to plan. The march of infantry, with heavy guns, light arms and armored units, was sent against the military air force base. Heavy artillery guns, .105-calibre, rattled past in their trucks; showers of machine gun fire from the attacking planes was ignored. These guns took up their predetermined positions in the hills around the airport.

Meanwhile, two aviators arrived in a jeep at the doors of the guard of honor, as emissaries of the rebels, to impose conditions of surrender. They stated that the entire air force was united and determined to reduce all loyal military installations to dust. Instead of meeting Colonel Cahueque, commander of the guard of honor, who was busy leading the troops in carrying out "Operation Whip," they came face to face with the President himself.

These men were not in the least humble, but certainly not as arrogant with the President as they would have been with a commanding officer. They saw it was impossible to threaten me, and instead of considering their conditions I sent them back to their rebel leaders with the message that within five minutes our heavy artillery would start to destroy the field, the planes, and the military installations they were temporarily holding. I said that the only acceptable terms were unconditional surrender. Shaken, they departed.

I then left the barracks and personally inspected the gun emplacements that were hidden in a small wood from which only a small part of the city could be seen. The observation post was high on a hill, more than 1,000 feet away, but from this position the observers had a perfect view of the military airport. The firing had already commenced and they were hitting the field with their first shots—quite a record to make a hit at 8,000 feet, directed only by the instructions of an observation post. Well aimed! Meanwhile, the Mariscal Zavala Brigade Headquarters, one and one-half miles distant, began to fire on the field with .75's, and at this great distance they made direct impact on a C-47 which was ready to take off and put it out of commission while it was being fueled.

When the insurrectionists felt the impact of our accurate fire they boarded a C-47 transport and took off so violently and with such fear that they forgot to release the safety pin on the carriage and could not retract their wheels. The infantry and the armored units advanced on the field. The ground troops charged on the air force installations and met some resistance from machine gun fire.

The traitorous attack had begun at 9:30 in the morning, and it was but two hours later, at 11:30 A.M. that they surrendered, raising a white flag.

I can only say that I am grateful to the Almighty for having spared my loved ones, and my own life which He has seen fit to sustain during these years of crisis.

EPILOGUE

THIS story must remain incomplete.

Not only has it been impossible to describe completely all the events within Guatemala, but it is also impossible to write "finis" to the story of my war with communism.

These years have been difficult years for all of humanity. We are in the midst of the greatest revolution the world has ever seen and the end is not in sight; all peoples must prepare for readjustments. There is no stemming the flood of change.

My war with communism has merely been the fight against destructive forces—forces that would destroy the hard-won achievements of mankind.

But there is no easy path. There is no quick solution to our economic and political problems, and anyone who says otherwise is either a fool or a demagogue.

This is our battle: to convince people that free enterprise, liberty, democratic institutions and representative government are the best answers to the elimination of poverty, want, and hardship, and to prove that the panaceas of communism are mere illusions.

But people do not always understand. The only position an honest man can take is to defend those things in which he believes.

And to humbly pray that he may be acting wisely.

INDEX

231

Date Due

Demco 293-5